Table of Contents

Asperger´s Syndrome (AS) is one of the autism spectrum disorders. Individuals with AS have little social interaction and have very poor communication skills. They often appear eccentric, weird or odd. Asperger's is now referred to as either Autism Spectrum Disorder or High Functioning Autism.

People with AS are incapable of feelings and empathy and because of their condition they are unable to see that they are lacking. Empathy is needed to connect people emotionally if you are to have a close relationship with someone an emotional connection is required.

To connect with someone you have to have an awareness of each other of each other's thoughts and feelings and you have to understand and care about them. If you do not express that you care and that you understand them there can be no real connection.

It is impossible to have a real connection with a person afflicted with Asperger's Syndrome. Their partners and children are invalidated, neglected, unseen, unheard and unknown. Because of this their partners and children suffer from extreme emotional neglect which results in significant emotional trauma.

Researchers researching AS and Autism have used MRI scans to study the brains of adults with AS which has revealed that they have significantly less white matter in the part of the brain which processes language and facial recognition and emotions. White matter is needed to connect different regions of the brain and allowing them to communicate with each other. The white matter in an AS brain is not there so the AS brain simply cannot understand facial expressions, humour, emotions, sarcasm in short they are lacking in the qualities needed to form and sustain relationships.

Asperger's is not treatable they won't get better there is no cure they are like this for life. It's not a personality disorder it's a neurological disorder the part of the brain which processes facial expressions, humour and feelings is simply not developed so no matter how hard you try they will not change or get better. There are no drugs or therapy to treat this condition the best you can hope if you want to stay in an AS/NT relationship is to form coping strategies and approaches for your partner and yourself

It is very difficult if not impossible to be in a relationship with someone with Asperger's as they are wired very differently to someone neuro typical (normal) they don't think like you or me and they don't mean to hurt you but they will.

I read somewhere that some people refer to someone with Asperger's as a Sperg; I thought this was really appropriate as it defines them as an alien which to all intents and purposes this is how they appear.

4

I lived for 13 years with an undiagnosed AS partner and the problems with the relationship crept up on me and AS revealed itself bit by bit. AS is called an invisible disability as it's not something you can see and it's not obvious to begin with. The issues were invisible to begin with neither myself or my ex was aware of the condition and so it remained undiagnosed until I started to research why he behaved so oddly and coldly

After I diagnosed my partner (most Asperger's individuals are diagnosed by their spouses as they after all see the full picture) you would think it would have given me peace of mind that I wasn't crazy after all, but it didn't, it made me angry that I had had to live through this nightmare and that I had been so damaged by the experience.

If I had have known he had AS I would not have chosen to stay with him so long after all I wouldn't consciously have chosen to share my life with someone so incredibly selfish, so negative, so emotionally destructive. Would I or would you?

Having spent years with a gut feeling that something was very wrong in my relationship but never being able to put my finger on what it was, I finally decided that I could not take any more of this emotional pain and that enough was enough and that I couldn't and wouldn't take it any longer.

My ex and I had the same discussions and arguments about the same problems for years and this had taken its toll on me and left me feeling very isolated and alone. I had to give up on the relationship for my own sanity and for the sanity of our son.

My ex had a complete inability to deal with any emotional aspect of our relationship and simply could not cope with the needs of our child. When I came across Asperger's, wow! For years what had not made sense to me suddenly did the light bulb moments went ping ping ping and everything that had confused me and left me feeling bewildered for years suddenly made sense.

If you have an AS spouse they will destroy you, they don't mean to but whether they mean to or not they will. If I ran over you and killed you with my car and it was a terrible unfortunate accident, you are still dead, I didn't mean to kill you but I did.

I must point out that all people are different including all Asperger's individuals. We are all shaped by our parents, background, friends, family, where we live and our life experiences and in addition to this if someone does have Asperger's it will depend on where they are

6

on the spectrum. This book is not meant as a formal diagnosis but it will give you a good idea if your partner does have AS. My ex had most of the traits listed in this book but your partner does not have to have ALL of them to have Asperger's. If you suspect that your partner does have AS he or she will have to go to a specialist to be diagnosed formally.

You must be puzzled over your partner's behaviour to be reading this book right now. I do hope this book helps you understand your partner better and if you do get a diagnosis hopefully there might be time to save the relationship before it goes too rotten to save.

Remember it is very possible that someone can go their whole life and never know that they have Asperger's. Asperger's syndrome has only really been recognised over the past 25 so there are many people out there who have not been diagnosed.

Reciprocity will be difficult or impossible with someone with Asperger's. An emotional bond is hard to develop and maintain if one partner in the relationship believes that they are superior in some way. My ex ASOH (Asperger's Other Half) treated me like a silly little girl it was more like a parent and child relationship. He genuinely thought that it was me that had the problems he said that he didn't understand why I was so up and down and he was always on a level.

In my relationship with my now ex AS partner I was puzzled why he could be so seemingly emotional and perfect when I was dating him and literally overnight he changed into this silent distant man. I was puzzled until I read one of Tony Atwood books and this paragraph stood out to me:

The person with Asperger's Syndrome may have developed a superficial expertise in romance and dating from careful observation, and by mimicking actors and using the script from television programs and films… Some partners have explained that they never saw the real person before they were married, and after their wedding day, the person abandoned the persona that was previously so attractive."

(Tony Atwood, The complete Guide to Asperger's Syndrome)

My ASOH was wonderful when I was dating him I fell head over heels in love with this lovely man, I couldn't believe my luck in meeting someone so thoughtful and sweet. As soon has he moved in it changed OVERNIGHT.

Once he had moved in with me he became a silent stranger he never showed me any emotion at all but I honestly thought that one day I would break through the "wall" I thought he had erected. It took me years to realise that it wasn't a wall at all it was just him he simply did not feel emotions like I did.

If your partner does indeed had AS (Asperger's) he will display few emotions the only emotions my ASOH displayed was anger and indifference. How can you create a loving partnership with someone who can't show you any emotion?

Is your partner completely unmoved by emotional events or movies? My ex ASOH didn't give a toss when the cat which had lived next door to us for 10 years died. The cat was called Eric and he was such a sweet little thing he would run up to us both every day for us to stroke him. I was really upset when he died but to my ex he was just a smelly animal. He didn't show any emotion at Eric's death or sad films or sad events or even when I lost my dad. My ex didn't show any happy emotions either even when our beautiful little boy was born, to him it was just another day.

Emotions are very important part of a relationship they are critical for humans, neuro typical humans (not autistic) need emotions we need emotional validation.

Studies have shown that monkeys who do not receive affection die they literally wither and die. Humans who do not receive affection and emotion tend to isolate themselves or have very poor esteem if their emotional needs are not met.

Often we aren't aware that our emotional needs are not being met but we know that something is missing.

Our emotional needs are:

To feel as though we are listened to and understood.
To feel loved and respected
To feel appreciated
To feel valued
To feel accepted
To feel supported
We need to give and receive affection
We need to be shown love
We need conversation and companionship

Think of a child growing up and imagine that its parents give it all it needs materially but emotionally they give nothing to their child. The child is going to try and get some attention from its parents to validate that it is loved usually by being naughty as some attention is better than none. Just think of the damage being done to that child as it grows into an adult they are not going to form into a fully rounded adult, they are going to be missing a vital part of what is needed to be a well-balanced adult. Well-being with someone with AS is a little like the child scenario are you doing things to get attention off them to validate that they do actually love you?

With my ASOH (Asperger's other Half) I tried my best to get some attention from him I told him jokes to try and make him laugh, he told me I wasn't funny I was just silly. I tried to be the best wife I could, keeping myself attractive, keeping the house nice, being the best mum I could but nothing worked I felt like I was invisible to him. I tried to connect with him for years to no avail, but as I was not aware of AS at the time I carried on trying thinking one day that I would connect with him that he would see me and love me. I now know it was a waste of effort as he was not capable of connecting with me or anyone for that matter.

If our emotional needs are not met this can sometimes lead to addiction to cover the emotional pain we feel or infidelity as we try to get some love and recognition elsewhere as we are not receiving the love we need at home.

1. Does your partner meet your emotional needs?

2. Do they show you any emotion?

3. Do they downplay the importance of emotions, approaching matters in a cool logical way?

4. Do they show excitement about anything?

5. Do they show any warmth to you?

6. Do you KNOW that they love you or are you not sure?

7. Can you connect with your partner emotionally?

I never really knew that my ex ASOH loved me; he said he loved me but the words always seemed empty without meaning. I used to think to myself "he must love me he has stayed with me for years; he wouldn't have stayed if he didn't love me".

My ex ASOH said he loved every day but he didn't behave like he loved me, in fact he behaved like he didn't really like me. I used to ask him how he felt about me and he used to say "I love I am here aren't I?"

I used to feel puzzled whether he did love me or not, he was here living with me, but everything seemed superficial and top surface there was never any intimate conversations and really deep talks. He said the words "I love you" but he didn't mean them. I always felt like I was an annoyance to him, in the way and that he just put up with me. I used to think to myself that if we split up he would not feel a thing, he would just move on to the next housekeeping relationship, and as long as his meagre needs were met it didn't matter who met them. If I said anything to him he just said that I was unstable.

When we split it proved to me that he didn't love me that I was right all along. He moved on straight away, I was replaced without a thought, I meant nothing, I had not even caused a ripple on his pond.

13

Like a square peg in a round hole, oh yes this one fits my ASOH (Asperger's Other Half) perfectly he never fit in anywhere he was always regarded as odd or weird. He HATED school and would do anything to get out of it. When he was at primary school his mom told me that he didn't have any friends and he always used to play on his own.

His mom also told me that when he was little he had a box of toy cars which he took everywhere with him. They went on holiday and forgot to take these cars with them his mom told me he screamed that much that his dad had to get back in the car drive 300 miles and pick up the box of cars, once he had his cars he was happy.

My ex ASOH didn't fit in at high school either when he attended high school he hated it and again he very few friends. One of the teachers once had him held up by the throat shouting at him telling him he was a weirdo. The teacher in question was sacked.

As a child he didn't fit in with the other kids in the neighbourhood and he never played out with the other kids in the street he preferred to stay in his loft bedroom playing with plastic toy soldiers.

He attended cubs but hated that too and once again he was on his own not bonding or forming relationships with his peers. His parents made him go to cubs to try and get him out of his bedroom for a while but he did not want to attend he preferred his own company.

As a teenager he didn't have girlfriends and he didn't go out with other kids his age he preferred to be in his bedroom playing video games. While other teenagers were out exploring life, my ex stayed in his room on his own.

When my ex ASOH started work he started an apprenticeship with an engineering firm and he was very good at his job as it was all logical. His mom and dad worked at the same place and his mom told me that when P (I shall refer to him as P from this point forward) used to walk into the canteen where his mom worked all the girls used to say to each other here is P isn't he gorgeous and his mom laughed as she said he was completely oblivious to the attention he got from the other sex.

Despite P being very handsome he didn't have the conversation or the social skills to talk to girls and he did not have his first girlfriend until he was 20, and guess what she picked him and did all the running.

P had many jobs over the years and he never fit in anywhere, he was not happy with any of his jobs. He used to come home and moan and moan about everyone at work he used to say they were all idiots and they didn't know what they were doing. Nothing was his fault, of course it was everyone else's fault that things were not going right for him.

P was made redundant from every job he had he was made redundant 8 times in 12 years.

I used to feel very protective of P as he really wasn't a bad man he was just a man that didn't fit in and didn't have very good social skills and I wanted to save him from the big bad world.

If P and I used to go anywhere new he was a bit like a fish out of water and he used to stiffen and use very formal manners to get by. Unlike me you wouldn't find him chatting to any one he didn't know and often when I had been chatting to someone he would say "who is that" to which I often replied "I don't know I just got talking to her in the que"

Some individuals with AS will talk and talk for ages on subjects they are interested in and if the other person glazes over with boredom they will not notice this and they will carry on talking. Someone with AS will not

16

notice the facial expressions and the little hints that the person is bored and they will carry on pontificating. Also they are so interested and fascinated with their topic they are not aware that the subject that they are interested in could be incredibly uninteresting to someone else. If someone normal was boring someone in a conversation they would usually see this and change the subject or give the other person a chance to talk.

Some individuals with Asperger's are a little like Mr Spock of Star Trek they are very logical and will not speak if they have nothing to say. They can't make small talk and conversations with them are usually one sided they might just give one word answers making it impossible to have a sustained conversation.

Trouble is conversations are a necessity for a good relationship and if you are in a relationship with someone with AS you will find it very difficult to get close to that person as you will not receive any affection and or a two way conversation.

My ex simply did not speak unless it was to criticise or moan or give me an order to do something. It was like living in a house with Mr Spock we were just distant housemates who shared a house, child, and bank account and had sex occasionally.

17

My ASOH (Asperger's Other Half) was not at all socially adept he was very socially awkward he did not like to be around crowds, he didn't like parties unless they were very small and he knew the people. He never came to families parties with me I was always on my own. There were many social occasions what we attended together but from which he departed after a short while. He simply did not need the social interaction that I did.

Sometimes he would make an effort if he liked the person and he did like one of my friends and her husband so he would come to their BBQ's and dinner parties but he wouldn't have much to say, as I can talk a dead man round (my son who was 10 said that to me) it wasn't really noticed and it was put down to him just being quiet.

He didn't like people calling at the house unannounced and when they did he would either not greet then at all or greet them awkwardly and disappear upstairs to leave the guests to me.

My social life deteriorated bit by bit I really didn't notice it as it happened so gradually. I did think when I first started to date him that he would come out of his shell the more time he spent with me, as I am a very sociable chatty person but he didn't, instead my world shrank to his as he was not capable of change.

1. Does your man not fit in anywhere?

2. Did your partner struggle in school was they bullied or did they not have many friends?

3. Does your partner seem like a fish out of water in new situations?

4. Does your partner struggle with people at work?

Poor Social Skills

They have great difficulty in understanding social situations and other people's thoughts and feelings.

Impaired social interactions are a key indicator that someone has Asperger's syndrome it's one of the most striking features of AS. If you partner does have AS then they probably appear to be social disconnected or simply not that interested in socialising with people. They might socialise a little but their social cup is full after a short while.

If you are curious about your partner and have begun to ask questions about his or her behaviour as you know something is not right this trait alone doesn't mean that your partner definitely has AS. If he or she does not display some of the other core indicators and only displays this one, then the chances are that they do not have AS.

If your partner is warm and compassionate and they show love and affection but they are not very good socially then they probably don't have AS. If however they have difficulty in social situations and display a number of the other elements of AS then the chances are that they do have AS. Please remember this is not a formal diagnosis.

People with AS often find it difficult to develop and sustain friendships with their peers as they cannot understand nonverbal communication such as facial expressions and eye contact. They seldom show affection towards others and they sometimes come across as rude, ignorant and stand offish.

P wasn't interested in socialising and could go for months without going out or seeing anyone apart from going to work and apart from seeing me and our son, with whom he spent little time with. He did not have many friends and he could not sustain friendships.

The only friend he maintained a relationship with was one friend he played on the X-box with and it wasn't really a friendship they just shared a common interest, which was the X-Box and they both, were obsessive about car racing like the Grand Prix.

When we went to any parties he did not socialise easily with any of my friends or family he looked stiff and awkward with them, luckily enough my friends and family are very friendly and they did try to put him at ease.

Not only did P have difficulty interacting with his peers he showed a complete lack of desire to do so. If we did go to any parties and I did go to lots of parties as I have a very large extended family P used to leave after a short time, usually with an excuse like he didn't feel well or he had a headache.

One Christmas a neighbour and friend invited us to go around on Christmas Eve and I accepted as we were not doing anything else just staying in (which was very boring for me and our son). P was not happy he did not want to go to this neighbours house party he wanted to stay in, when we got to the party he sat in a chair and would not move he would not speak to anyone he sat in the chair with a face like thunder. I was fuming with him he was so rude and when my neighbour introduced us to a couple who were the same age as us (and were potential friends) he refused to talk to them apart from to say hello.

P would never attend work parties; he said he spent all day with them why the hell did he want to go out with them too? We never attended a works Christmas party together as he didn't want to come to mine and he wouldn't attend his own works party.

P did not like to socialise too much and as I am social butterfly this drove me mad as I thought he was just rude and ignorant. My social life died bit by bit and as it was a gradual thing I didn't notice until it was all but gone.

1. Does your partner have trouble making friends?

2. Does your partner not particularly like social situations?

3. Is your partner awkward in social situations?

4. Has your social life deteriorated?

Black and white thinking there are no shades of grey with AS thinking.

Black or white thinking where AS is concerned is quite complicated to explain. With my ASOH he was right and you were wrong and that was that. I used to try and to put my point of view across but he would not change his mind, he was right and I was wrong.

I always think that in any situation with two people that there is their point of view and there is your point of view and then there is the truth. People see things differently they often see them as they are and not how it is.

People with AS see things how they see them and as far as they are concerned that's it that is how it is and they simply will not change their mind. They do not have the capacity to see things from anyone else's point of view.

Let me give you an example. We were out once and there was a homeless guy who looked like he was an alcoholic he was a bit of a mess. I am soft and I felt really sorry for him as I always think that you don't know what his life has been like and you don't know what drove him to be like this. I gave him a couple of quid and P went mad at me the conversation went like this:

P: "he is just going to go and buy some booze now you idiot".

Me: I said you don't know that he might need something to eat the poor buggar"

P: It's his own fault he should clean up and get a job.

Me: You don't know why he is like this he might have gone through hell and back.

P: Well he chose to drink he could stop and clean up.

Me: If it was that easy don't you think he would have done that?

P: Course it's easy just have a flaming wash and get a job, or go on benefits or something.

Me: Don't be so stupid if it was easy for him don't you think he would do it or have done it already? Do you honestly think he wants to live like that?

P: It's you being stupid he is a down and out.

Me: I give up end of subject.

P: Just because I am right.

Me in my head: I could strangle him.

With P things were right or things were wrong there was no in-between at all. One of my neighbours was a bit of a criminal and he used to get knocked off stuff all the time, one Christmas he got a load of Armani perfume and it was really cheap. I told P I was going to buy some for Christmas presents but he went mad and said I couldn't buy it as it was stolen. I said I know it's a bit naughty but it will save us a fortune, NO he said you are not buying it its stolen and it's wrong to buy it. I didn't buy it.

Sometime later the same neighbour had some knocked off X-box games and P bought some for himself. I said what are you buying them for they are stolen and you went mad at me when I was going to get that perfume. He said it's save us fifty quid (£).

I was once telling P that I friend of mine was leaving her husband.

P: He is a nice guy?

Me: He is a bastard with her she is really unhappy.

P: He is ok with her when I have seen him, he is a nice fella.

26

Me: He goes out drinking all the time and he is really controlling with her she can't do anything but he can do what he wants and she is sick of it.

P: Well he has been alright with me.

Me: So what you are not married to him.

P: (he had to get the last word in) Well he seems nice enough to me.

Me: (in my head) I give up why I not learn there is no arguing with you.

With P you were either nice or you were a dickhead.

Another friend of mine rang P and asked him about a fella that P worked with as her cousin had started to date him. P said tell her to keep away from him he is right dickhead and he has had a fight with a co-worker he's an absolute idiot. They are now very happily married and have been for 5 years.

P hated his sister and when I asked why he said she was horrible to me when we were kids, when I enquired what had she actually done to him it was just sibling fighting but he held a grudge against her which he never dropped. I told him that if I or my sister had held a grudge against each other for all the horrible stuff we did to each other we would have never spoke to each other again.

I remember on occasion when my sister was getting on my nerves she was teasing me about something so I drew glasses and moustache on all her posters with a big black marker, in retaliation she scribbled all over my fairy stickers I had stuck on my wardrobe.

There was a time we were arguing and she threw a pair of scissors at me and broke the foot off an antique porcelain doll an old lady had given to me so I punched her, and this is just a couple of examples of our fighting but I love her dearly, guess what? We grew up and realised that kids do this kind of stuff.

1. Ask yourself does your partner have rigid thinking?

2. Once your partner has made up their mind is it impossible to change it?

3. Is your partner thinking very black and white?

Complete inability to see something from someone else's perspective.

People with AS usually have a complete inability to see or understand or recognise a different perspective. They cannot even acknowledge the very possibility that there may be other perspectives apart from their own.

There's always more than one point of view but someone with AS think that things are one way and that's it. They cannot understand that their point of view is just that their point of view they do not understand that there are other points of view. Of course this makes communication very difficult with them as they cannot see someone else's perspective.

The inability to see things from another's perspective is a big problem if you are in a relationship with someone with AS and it also causes problems with work. To someone with AS things are the way they are and that it's that and if you think differently you are wrong.

I am quite spiritual and I do believe in life after death that's my point of view and that's what I believe. I can see that this might be odd or strange to someone who is logical or scientific but I don't ram my spirituality down

29

people's throat and if they think differently that's fine by me they are entitled to their opinion.

When my father passed away suddenly I was devastated and I did not want to believe that I would not see him again ever, so I read every spiritual book I could. I read an excellent book about a nurse who worked in the HDU (high dependency unit for seriously ill patients) and she had spoken to several people who had died and then been resuscitated. The patients she spoke to who had died and been brought back to life by modern medicine had told her about crossing over to the other side and being sent back as it was not their time yet. At first she was sceptical and then she decided to research life after death the result was a book and it was fascinating it was called "The wisdom of near death experiences" I loved the book.

P didn't believe in life after death he said it was bullshit. I tried to tell him my point of view and gave him some examples but he said "it's bullshit when you are dead you are dead".

I had a boyfriend years ago who I loved very much but for a number of reasons we broke up and then we got back together and we broke up again and finally we broke up for good. I had not seen this boyfriend for about 16 years when one night I had a very vivid dream

30

that he was looking for me. He was shouting my name and someone in my dream said "Katy, Nick is looking for you". I said "where is he" and then he was there coming towards me holding out his arms, into which I ran to hug him. He said "I have come to say goodbye to you" I said "Aww please don't go" "He replied "I have to I have just come to say goodbye, I have a picture of you in my wallet and I take it out every day and kiss it, why did you not come back for me?" I just looked at him as he waved goodbye and then he was gone.

I woke up and straight away I knew he was dead and he has come to say goodbye to me. I drove to work that morning with Nick on my mind and as soon as I got into work I turned on the computer and googled his name. I found his obituary in his local newspaper online it mentioned his dad and his sister so I knew it was him. I found his niece on Facebook and sent her a message which read:

Hi Keeley

You probably don't remember me but I went out with your uncle Nick years ago. I have heard he has passed please tell me it's not true.

Katy xx

She wrote back almost straight away:

Hi Katy

I do remember you; you were very nice to me and let me sit on your knee. I am sorry but its true Nick took his own life two weeks ago.

Keeley xx

There is no one on God's green earth telling me that Nick did not come to say goodbye, why after all those years should I dream about him and it be true?

I told P about my dream and subsequent findings and he said it was just a dream. I said but it was so specific and real, he said it's just a coincidence and life after death is bullshit.

I remember one incident which puzzled me at the time but now makes sense now I know my ex had AS. Me and my now ex ASOH and another couple were watching the film "The Butterfly Effect" and how the main character could go back in time and change one small detail, and then return to the present. By changing that one small detail things had massively changed when he returned to the present.

After the film we were all discussing how we would like to go back into the past and change things or if certain things had not happened where we would be now. I said if I had not met P that our son wouldn't have been born. P was really puzzled he said of course he would have been born, I asked how could he have been born if I had not met you. He just could not get his head around that things would be totally different for both of us if we had not met. I kept trying to explain to him but in the end I gave up, he just could not see it.

P was very militant with our son and he really didn't need to be as Adam was and still is a very good boy. I used to say to P you don't have to order him just ask him and he will do it, like for instance he would say to Adam "up to bed now" I said you just have to say "bedtime sunshine" and he will say OK mummy or OK daddy. P used to get this awkward look on his face as if to say I'm right and your wrong and he would carry on barking orders at our small son. He just couldn't see it from my perspective that you didn't need to bark orders, you just needed to ask nicely. P thought that children should be seen and not heard so he had a very strict way of dealing with Adam. I believe that children should be able to grow and have their own opinion. Don't get me wrong if Adam was out of line I wasn't too much of a pushover and I would punish him.

1. Ask yourself is your partner able to see that there are different ways of looking at something?

2. Is your partner able to see things from your perspective?

3. Does your partner think they are right and you are wrong?

They sometimes say something without considering the emotional impact on the listener.

Some AS individuals are very honest and do not have the social filter of a Neuro Typical (NT – Normal) and sometimes can say what they are thinking without how this will be received. If someone asked an NT do you think I look fat in this they would think for a moment and come up with an answer which would not offend the other person, maybe something like "no you don't' look fat but I have seen you in more flattering outfits". Someone with AS doesn't have this filter they would probably say "yes you look really fat in it" they are unaware that this could be hurtful.

Someone with AS will not think twice about criticising you or someone else and they either don't understand it can hurt or they don't care that it will hurt. Their tolerance for ideas that are different from their own is practically non-existent this makes them argumentative. I'm sure that if they did understand the upset that they caused they would not continue.

AS individuals don't seem to have the filter that a neuro typical (normal) person has and will just say it as it is. My ex ASOH had learned over the years to keep quiet rather than blurt out was he thought. He had learned that it upset people so it was better to just keep quiet; it was one of his coping mechanisms to function in the normal world.

I would ask him did he like my hair up and he would say no it's not nice I don't like trussed up hair. I would ask him if I looked a bit fat in a dress and he would say yes you should go back to the gym. He was brutally honest when I first met him but after him upsetting me many times he then wouldn't say anything.

Another example was I asked him did he like my new dress and he said no its fow (a British word for horrible). I remember once being sat on a stool in a hotel room with my short pyjamas on and he said what are those lumps on your legs? Cheers how to make a girl feel loved! I wouldn't mind I was so slim and toned at the time and I had very little cellulite but it made me feel very upset so when I got home I threw my short pyjamas in the bin.

My ex ASOH was ALWAYS criticising me I really could not do right for doing wrong. The way I drove was wrong, the way I parked my car was wrong, the way I put the cutlery away in the draw was wrong, the way I put the shopping away was wrong, they Christmas presents I bought Adam were shit, the helmet I bought for Adam for

his bike was wrong it made him look stupid.
EVERYTHING I did was wrong.
I would be telling someone a story and if I got one minute detail wrong he would pick me up "No that's not right it was like this blah blah" it made it look as though I was telling lies. So the way I told a story was wrong…..

He didn't think about the impact it would have on me saying the things he did.

When someone is constantly negative to you they are hurting you whether they realise it or not. This constant stream of hurtful energy will interfere with your self-esteem and self-worth which will eventually change who you are and how you look at the world around you. I know it has with me I am a lot more negative than I used to be, it's something I am working on.

1. Does your partner not have a filter and say things that may hurt?

2. Does your partner constantly criticise you?

3. Is your partner completely unaware why they have hurt you?

Nope no spontaneity at all none whatsoever no ad-hoc walks or going to the cinema at the last minute, no holidays booked on a whim, no BBQ's planned on the spur of the moment, nada, zero, nought, nothing!

I am very spontaneous as I don't really like planning anything, someone might ask me what I am doing a week on Friday and my answer would be "I don't know what I am doing in an hour never mind next Friday".

I got up one morning and decided I wanted a new car I wanted a Nissan Juke.

Nissan Juke

I rang my mother and said "mum I have seen a car and I want it do you fancy a ride to see it"? My mum said "you are just like your dad talk about making your mind up and then doing it". Off we went to see this car I wanted and I loved it, I loved everything about it, so I bought it. The following day I drove it home.

I decided I wanted a dog so I googled Shih Tzu and found a gorgeous little dog I picked him up the next day.

My son called him Bobby and we have now had him for four years, he is delightful and much loved.

Bobby

Sometime an idea will pop into my head like I just fancy an ice cream so I will jump up and drive to the shopping centre where they sell loads of different flavour ice creams and have my spur of the moment ice cream.

If your partner has AS there will be nothing spontaneous at all. Don't expect spontaneous sex either, my ex and I had sex on a Saturday morning. Oh yes Saturday morning how boring is that? If I did try and pounce on him spontaneously I would get rejected, so I stopped trying as I didn't want to keep getting rejected.

I would suggest a weekend away; let's go to the lakes this weekend we are not doing anything? My suggestion would be rejected. Shall we go to the cinema tonight, my suggestion would be rejected. Let's go for a ride out to Blackpool and get some chips? He would reply with something negative like "Blackpool is a shit hole full of scrotes" (British word for trailer trash). My every suggestion would be rejected, so guess what I gave up. He had an automatic no reflex to everything. Everything I suggested was kyboshed by him, I gave up suggesting things and did more and more on my own or with Adam.

Don't expect any spontaneity from your ASOH they are not capable of spontaneity and they don't really appreciate it off you either.

One bright sun shining Sunday I said to my ASOH lets have a barbeque the weather is amazing today let's make the most of it? If you lived in the north of England you would know that sunshine is not a regular occurrence and you have to make the most of the few days' sunshine we get.

My ASOH didn't want a BBQ he didn't like me organising spontaneous events so he said no. I was determined to have BBQ so Adam could have some fun with my friends kids and we could have some good company (which I was crying out for). I invited my friends most of which

40

were thrilled at a spontaneous event and then I got all the BBQ stuff from the local supermarket.

I set up the water slide and paddling pool for the children and set up a separate table for the kid's food. A few friends arrived with their kids and I shouted for P to come down and join in the fun and he said I told you I didn't want a BBQ. He didn't come down for the whole day, I could see my friends were a little upset by this but what could I do?

The children had a fantastic time sliding on the water slide and jumping straight from the trampoline into the paddling pool but again I was alone.

If it was a nice Saturday I would say to my ASOH shall we drive to the beach with Adam and take a pick nick? "No I am not driving this weekend I have drove hundreds of mile this week" I said "I will drive", "no I don't want to go my hay fever is bad". Why oh why did I carry on trying?

He didn't cope with anything unexpected or was not in his plan or routine, he said no to almost everything I suggested his automatic reflex action was NO.

1. Does your partner ever do anything spontaneous or does everything have to be planned?

2. Has your partner got a strong NO reflex?

3. Does your partner reject your spontaneous suggestions?

Not at all interested in sharing experiences with others.

P (My ASOH) was not at all interested in sharing any of his experiences with me or anyone else, he came home from work and he didn't really talk about his day unless it was to moan about someone. I did try my best to extract some conversation out of him as I really didn't know about AS and I was not specifically looking for it, I kept on trying thinking I would one day break through and we would be able to share our inner worlds.

I would ask P about his day and he would just pull a face as if to say it was crap, so I would ask if anything interesting had happened and he just shrugged his shoulders as if to say no, I would then ask had he been out for lunch and he would say three words like "just to Asda" (Asda is a supermarket in England). I would then ask if he would like a cup of tea and he would say "OK" he never said yes he always said OK.

Then he would disappear upstairs for ages until I shouted him for tea. I sometimes would get angry with him for disappearing and would shout to him "are you coming down". Sometimes he would reluctantly come down and sometimes he made an excuse not to come down. I did not know that this time alone after work was a sign of AS that they need to time to diffuse from trying to act normal all day.

P would never tell me stories of when he was a child or a teenager and he never mentioned his ex-girlfriend, which I found odd as I called my ex-boyfriend not fit to burn and I was always telling him about stuff from when I was child and stories from when I was a bit of a wild party girl when I was younger. He didn't tell me one story about his childhood I just gleaned information from his mother and his sister (when he was still talking to his sister).

I would ask him about his childhood but he gave me scant information, I asked him about his ex-girlfriend and again he gave me scant information saying that she wasn't important now.

P once went to America with work and Adam and I stayed at home P was away for 2 weeks, he rang me twice. In the couple of times he rang me it was me talking and him listening, I asked him about America, "it's alright I don't see much I am in work". My god getting a conversation out of him was painful I was glad he didn't ring much.

P never wanted to spend any time with me or Adam he preferred being alone and his hobbies were solitary, like cycling and running. He wasn't bothered about sharing

44

his time or any past or present experiences with me or anyone else.

P wasn't the slightest bit interested in my day and he would never ask if I had had a good day or even anything about my day. He didn't ask what I had been doing or where I had been or if I had seen anyone. P didn't ask about Adam or how he was getting on at school. P wouldn't ever talk to Adam unless it was to bark orders to him or occasionally he would play on the X-box with him, he was totally disconnected from his little family.

P didn't interact in family life at all I didn't have the pleasure of enjoying my little family like normal marriages P just lived with us not talking not interacting it was all one sided from me. As he didn't share anything of his life I began to felt like we were just housemates.

My parents lived part of the time in a lovely house in Tenerife where the weather is hot all year. In all the time that I was with P he went to Tenerife once, once in nearly 13 years. Crazy really as we only had to book cheap flights and we could have gone for a long weekend here and there but he never wanted to go.

I started to go to Tenerife just with my little boy and leave P at home. When we were away he wouldn't ring me and if I rang him he wouldn't ask about my day or about my parents or even about his own son. When he picked me up from the airport it was like I had booked a taxi driver to come and get me and Adam as P showed no excitement or even interest in either of us. We would sit in the car on the way home from the airport in complete silence or with me inanely chattering away to fill the empty awkward silence.

If we were driving out anywhere I would comment on things like how beautiful the trees were at this time of year or say look at that church it looks so old, just general chit chat but P never commented on anything. If we were watching a film I would comment on the plot or the characters but P never did he just told me to shut up that I was bugging him.

P didn't have any plan for the future I would say to him "where do you see yourself in five years"? He would say "here with you and Adam". I would say to him "Don't you fancy something else something to look forward to"? "No I like it here". People with AS simply don't need to share their inner worlds with anyone and they don't want to share your inner world either.

1. Does your partner talk about his past experiences?

2. Is your partner interested in how your day has been?

3. Does your partner talk about his day?

4. Does your partner participate in family life?

5. Do you and your partner have a joint hobby?

6. Is your partner interested in hearing about your hobby?

7. Does your partner make general comments on everyday life?

Special Interests

They often have restricted interests or special interests like the computer or in my case the x-box.

People with AS often have limited interests and or solitary interests which don't involve anyone else like cycling or running.

P had very restricted interests where as I was interested in so many different things and I still am. P interests were limited to the X-box, running, cycling and keeping the house absolutely pristine.

When P started to get interested in running (as he didn't want to pay for a gym membership) he got obsessed with it really quickly and he went running every night whether it was raining, freezing or boiling. He wanted all the best gear and he researched the best running shoes the best running jacket he wanted the best of everything.

P spent ages researching and purchasing all the correct gear for his debut into running, he paid a fortune for the trainers, socks, jackets, running shorts. All his expensive purchases came out of a joint bank account into which I deposited the lion's share of the money. I thought if you went running you put on a pair of tracksuit bottoms your trainers and you were off! But no P had all the best gear with no expense spared.

Every single night he would come home from work get into his running gear set some app on his phone up and off he went. I suggested going with him one night but he said that I would be too slow and I would just hold him back. I got sick to death of his obsessive running and asked him could he not at least take one day off from his running as it would be nice to actually have tea as a family one night? No was the answer.

The running was starting to take a toll on P's body he kept straining some ligament or muscle in his leg and he would sit there rubbing it and complaining and then go running? He decided to start cycling instead as it would be easier on his body, so the research for cycling started then. Hours spent on the computer looking for the best bike, the best cycling shorts the best of everything again.

I wasn't very happy with him as I had been suggesting for ages that we all get bikes and go cycling together as a family and he said "I don't like cycling and I have never had a bike". But now it suited him he suddenly developed a liking for cycling.

When P had done his research and bought all the gear I told him he could piss off if he thought he was going to spend £2000 on a bike. He had said we couldn't afford to go on holiday but he could afford to spend £2000 on a bike?

P took out a loan in his name and bought his specialist bike which came all the way from Germany, he said it was the best as it was from Germany. When he had built his bike he became obsessed with cycling and he went every single night and every weekend off cycling on his own. I suggested that we could all go cycling as a family and he pulled his face as he said that we would hold him up. I wasn't very happy and I told him so, he didn't like confrontation so he held his hand up to my face and walked off and went upstairs.

P went away and he must have thought about it, he knew I would not wear a helmet as I am vain (I know it's silly of me) and it would spoil my hair and he knew this. He came downstairs and the conversation went like this:

P: I will go cycling with you if you wear a helmet.

Me: I am not wearing a helmet and you know I won't.

P: Well what if you fall off?

Me: I am not planning falling off thank you.

P: If you don't wear a helmet I am not going with you.

Me: It's not up to you to decide if I wear a helmet or not.

50

P: I am not going with you if you don't wear one simple as that.

Me: P I don't want to wear a helmet but I would like us all to go cycling together, don't be so anal about this.

P: You heard what I said.

Then off he went and we never did go cycling as a family and we never went running together.

I did some work for a company and they paid me in cash so I had about £1200 in cash. Me being a joker stuffed the money down my cleavage and said to P "get as much out with your teeth as you can and you can keep it". P just looked at me with a "don't be so stupid expression on his face". Then I said "let's go and do something daft with it like buy a 50 inch telly"? "No" he said "save it". A few days later he took the money up to the bank and paid off his bike loan with it.

Another one of P's special interests was the X-box he spent hours and hours on the damn thing. What made this even more isolating for me was the house that we lived in at the time was a three storey house with a large loft conversion.

The loft contained two rooms one was my office and the other room P had claimed for himself for his "play room". I asked him could I have the room as my workroom for my online shop as I needed a separate space to work, and even though my online selling contributed to the household income he would not hear of it.

The loft playroom housed a large sofa bed a very large television which was another one of P's selfish purchases; he bought a massive television for his X-box while Adam and I had a small old television downstairs. He bought it when plasma telly's first came out and he paid over £2000 for this television just for himself. Looking back I cannot believe how I put up with his selfishness for all those years.

P spent many hours up in that loft room playing games on his X-box while I was sat downstairs with Adam or on my own when Adam went to bed. I was very lonely.

The loneliness was biting I felt very isolated and unable to tell my friends and family as most of them thought he was a good man. It was such a stark contrast from when we were dating he was so lovely and kind, what the hell had happened to him what had I done to him to make him like this. I genuinely believed it was my fault that he behaved the way he did that I had done something to push him away. I started to research lack of feelings and

Asperger's came up top of the list. When I read about AS I was astounded this article was talking about P and then it clicked, I was his special interest in the beginning that's why he was so lovely. Once his special interest in me had waned he reverted to type.

1. Does your partner have special interests that they can get quite obsessed about?

2. Does your partner have limited interests?

3. Does your partner have solitary interests?

4. Were you a special interest to begin with?

P's speech was monotone and he had stock answers for a lot of things. What I mean by stock answers are answers he had stored up over the years and use where he though they would fit. When a normal person talks their voices rise and fall as they emphasise certain points or when they get excited about something P's tone didn't change much.

One thing that struck me about P was the way he greeted all his male friends and family. At first I thought it was just the way that all his friends greeted each other some daft thing they had conjured up between themselves. He would stiffly hold out his hand and shake their hand while saying "Hello Sir". He greeted his friends like this (they were few and far between) he greeted his dad like this, he greeted my dad this way in fact if they were male and no matter who they were P greeted them in this robotic way.

Sometimes as if trying to rectify this robotic speech P would put the inflection in the wrong place and it would sound odd, he would raise and lower his voice in the wrong place. Sometimes he would talk as though he was reading from a script and his voice would not vary where it should have varied.

1. Does your partner talk in a robotic way?

2. Does your partner have a monotone voice?

3. Does your partner add the inflection in the wrong places when he or she talks?

They can come across as pompous or arrogant.

Pompous means someone might appear to have excessive self-esteem or exaggerated dignity. We have all met pompous people who enjoy giving orders.

P came across as really pompous at times. In fact I remember when we had fallen out once and I had sent him a text in temper telling him he was a pompous pig.

He seemed to have a superiority complex, I don't know whether he did think he was superior but he definitely came across as though he did. Where ever he worked he thought everyone else was stupid and an idiot, he never thought it could be him.

With me he definitely thought he was superior and that I was a crazy person. I probably am a bit crazy but I am not stupid I taught adults computer software for years so I know I am quite clever but he made me feel stupid.

He would instruct me on how do things like for instance we were painting our front room with suede paint (paint that looks like suede once applied and dried) and of course he was applying the paint correctly and I wasn't. P then tried to teach me how do it correctly, I ignored him and carried on and do you know what my painting was nicer than his!

He was ALWAYS better at everything he did even down to putting the dishes in the dishwasher, he tried to instruct me how to put them in right. He treated me like a naughty wayward child who needed to be put back in line; it was more like a parent child relationship than a man and wife relationship.

1. Does your relationship feel like a parent child relationship?

2. Does it feel like your partner think he/she is superior?

3. Is everything you do wrong and they are right?

They don't get humour or sarcasm.

Humour

In order to understand jokes you have to have a certain level of understanding of non-verbal communication you need to be able to read other people's tone of voice, body language or facial expressions to be able to tell that they are joking. That is hard for someone with Asperger's as they cannot read facial expressions and they cannot read into other people's mental states so they don't get jokes or sarcasm.

That's not to say someone with AS does not find anything funny they do. P used to laugh out loud at the inbetweeners (very British humour) we both thought it was very funny and it was something we enjoyed together. He didn't find the comedy show Little Britain funny at all where I belly laughed at a lot of the scenes.

P could never tell I was joking he often said that I was taking the piss out of him, I wasn't I am very much a joker and I used humour to lighten situations this unfortunately didn't work with P. At the end of our relationship that he said he wanted someone normal and that I wasn't funny I was silly.

I remember one incident in particular which hurt my feelings as I was only trying to make him laugh. He was working upstairs in our loft office and I was downstairs on my own AGAIN. I was getting sick of him working (I know now that he was actively trying to avoid me as he had met someone else) so I sang at the top of my voice "All by myself don't wanna be all by myself". I waited to see if he responded, he didn't! I went upstairs and he was sat at the computer fuming. I was puzzled to why he was so angry; I said to him "did you not hear me singing to you"? He turned to face me and almost spat the words out "yes I flaming did, why are you taking the piss out of me he asked"? I was really really puzzled at his reaction to a joke, "I'm joking P I just wanted to make you laugh", P said "You are not joking you are taking the piss".

It didn't matter how many times I told him I was just joking he insisted I was taking the piss out of him. I wasn't I just wanted to make him laugh.

I am good at mimicking accents and sometimes I will switch to an American accent or a Liverpool accent to make someone laugh, P said he wished I wouldn't do that as it wasn't funny and I was crap at accents. Funny everyone had always told me that my accents were good and my little boy used to say to me "mummy talk in that Irish accent it make me laugh". Thank goodness my son is neuro typical.

I would often crack a joke with P but he didn't think I was funny even when everyone else laughed he remained stony faced. He once shouted me to come to the bathroom so I went upstairs to see what he was shouting about and he was stood there with the bathroom cupboard door open, glaring at me. I looked into the cupboard and there were about 20 empty toilet rolls in the cupboard (no-one ever changed the loo roll except me and no one ever used the large bathroom cupboard except me). "Yes" I said "what's the matter"? He pointed to the loo rolls and said "why haven't you put them in the bin that's ridiculous" I said "Adam is doing a project at school and I need to save 50 empty loo rolls for it". This was a complete lie I had made it up on the spot to make him laugh. He looked at me not knowing whether I was serious or not until I laughed and told him I had just made it up. He walked away stony faced and said "put them in the flaming bin". As usual I was left deflated.

When you tell a joke it's hard for someone with AS to tell whether you are joking or being serious in the first place, because they find reading into people's body language and tone difficult. If they can get past that and tell that the other person is joking they still might struggle to understand the joke as they understand the words according to their literal meanings and not according to some wordplay or double meaning.

60

As someone with AS is wired to use logic they may simply find the joke illogical and that it doesn't make any sense and therefore wouldn't find it funny.

Sarcasm

Sarcasm is the use of words that mean the opposite of what you really want to say especially in order to insult someone, to show irritation, or to be funny.

Similar to humour people with AS don't get sarcasm at they tend to take thing literally, they don't get the sarcastic tone in your voice or the sarcastic expression on your face, therefore they tend not to get sarcasm.

P didn't get sarcasm at all he took things I said literally like for instance I would say "isn't it beautiful out" when it was pouring it down. No he would say "it's raining"?

When something happened that we really didn't need like the washer breaking and flooding the kitchen I said "Great stuff that's just what I needed" He would pipe up with something like "what for the washer to flood the kitchen and then cough up 400 quid for a new washer"? "I am being sarcastic P" his reply was "well it's not funny". I didn't intend it being funny I was being sarcastic.

I am a very jokey person I was raised in a house where we were allowed to be who we were and humour and sarcasm were used a lot. P was brought up in a humourless household, a very strict household where humour was not used at all and everyone behaved very correctly. P's mum couldn't fart in front of his dad she would have to hold it in or go in another room. My dad would fart and shake his leg to make fun of it and we would laugh but be disgusted at the same time. P's family would have been horrified at this.

I am not saying that P didn't laugh at all but it was very rare and it was often put on.

Sometimes if P was moaning about something, which he did every day I would say "you're in a good mood aren't you?" He would look at me as though I was crazy and say "No I am flaming not are you taking the piss". I would tell him I was joking to lighten the mood, but he would say well you are not funny you are getting on my nerves.

1. Does your partner laugh at your jokes?

2. Do you and your partner laugh together with couples banter?

3. Does your partner take your jokes and sarcasm literally?

4. Does your partner think you are being stupid if you do something daft to make them laugh?

We all say daft things sometimes and we really don't mean them, if you said the daft thing to a normal person they would not take you seriously but if you say something to someone with AS they will take it literally as though you really mean it.

A common example of taking things literally is a child with AS being told to pull up their socks and actually bending down to this.

One man said his brother who had Asperger's that he was so frustrated that he was "pulling his hair out". He asked his brother had he really pulled some of his hair out although he had heard this expression before and he did know it was just an expression his brother didn't accompany the comment with a smile or a laugh so he thought he was serious. His brother had to explain to him that he had not really pulled out his hair.

One guy with AS was lifting something heavy and a co-worker joked and said that "someone's had porridge for his breakfast today" and the guy then proceeded to tell his co-worker that he had actually had toast for breakfast that morning.

When I was with my ex ASOH there were many examples of him taking me literally like for instance I was joking with him telling him he was special and then I added needs onto the end (special needs). P was not happy and he shot me a filthy look while saying in a very annoyed tone "huh if anyone is special needs here it's you". I said to him I was only joking P but he thought I was being nasty to him.

Another real life example of P taking things literally was when I had split up with P and then we had got back together. When we split I had put our house on the market and I had some trouble with an arrogant estate agent. I was fuming with this estate agent as she was incredibly rude to me and she shouted at me a couple of times when I wouldn't accept what I deemed to be an undervalued offer on the house.

When P and I had got back together we had took the house off the market and the estate agent had said that we still had to pay full fees. She had in her contract a clause stating that if we accepted an offer on the house and then we had withdrawn then she could by law charge us full fees. I had researched this clause and found several holes in her argument, one I had never signed a contract and two we had not accepted an offer on the house so therefore we could not have withdrawn from the offer as we didn't accept it in the first place.

I rang the estate agent and very calmly stated that we did not have to pay full fees and pointed out my arguments. She screamed at me down the phone (very professional don't you think) and said she would take us to court. I said calmly that she would be laughed out of court and she slammed the phone down on me.

I went to tell P what had happened and I was really annoyed at how she talked over me and was so incredibly rude. I said to P that I was going to take the estate agent board down from the front garden and put it in my car and take it to the estate agents office and throw it into the estate agents office. I said it with a smile as I was amused at my own joke, but P's reaction was to say "You can't do that you will end up getting arrested". I tried to explain to him that I was just angry and venting and that I wouldn't do that really but he thought I would.

Another example of my ex ASOH taking things literally was when a child at our son's school was bullying our son. I had spoken to the child's mother about her son bullying mine and her answer was boys will be boys and laughed. As you can well imagine I was furious as her child was a big fat lad and my son was a little slim lad he didn't stand a chance against the other child.

I was relating this story to my ex and I said I was going to slap the mother when I next saw her and again my ex took it literally and told me not to lose my temper and slap the mother of the bully (as if I would).

I knew I had to deal with this some way I couldn't have my son being bullied, I told the school the problem and they did absolutely nothing. I had a word with my son and told him never to start violence but next time the bully started to pick on him that he should kick the bully as hard as he could in the shins. When I went to pick my son up from school the teacher asked could she have a word with me, she then proceeded to tell me that my son had been sent to the naughty corner for kicking a child in the shins (the bully), I said to her "good". The teacher looked at me in horror and I said to her "my son has been bullied by that child for months and finally he has retaliated so I am proud of him". The teacher was again horrified as she said you don't treat violence with violence. I said I totally agree but the mother of the child did nothing and the school did nothing so what was my son to do? Keep on being bullied or retaliate and stop the bullying? I didn't punish my son I was proud of him for standing up to a bully.

I was telling my ex this story and just for a joke I added that the teacher was horrified at me for saying good and she gave me a disgusted look (she did) so I said to my ex "so I poked her in the eye". He looked at me and said "why the hell did you do that"?

Yet another example of taking things literally was when we were watching a very boring film it was so slow yawn! On the closing scene the main man was sat watching a sunset on his own having just had his long lost daughter visit him for the first time. I said to my ex "the next time she visits he will still be in the same place having been eaten by kangaroos" (it was set in New Zealand) and my ex said "he couldn't be eaten by kangaroos they don't have them in New Zealand" Dohhhhhh who cares I didn't mean it.

1. Does your partner take things literally?

2. Does your partner take your jokes or humour literally?

Flat Facial Expressions

They have few facial expressions.

Asperger's individuals have a "flat affect" this is a term which is used to describe the lack of facial expressions which someone with AS is likely to have.

With someone with AS expressive gestures are usually non-existent and there will be virtually no facial animation or vocal inflection. Someone with AS will have the flat affect and will have no or nearly none emotional expression. They will not react to circumstances that would arouse strong emotions in others.

NT's (neuro-typical, i.e. normal people) feel a range of emotions every day all day and this reflects in the facial expression that they display. For instance if I am thinking and puzzling over something I tend to frown, or if I am thinking about something nice I will smile, or if someone is bugging me I will raise my eyebrows and give them a dirty look.

My ex ASOH had very few facial expressions - apart from anger or misery or just total flatness. My ex would not respond to things that would have me in tears or would make me laugh. I would show him a picture of a puppy which I thought was cute and his face would not change at all. I would tell him a story of a child who had lost its parents and his face would not register any empathy it would remain the same or he would raise his eyebrows as though he knew he should react but didn't know how to.

We attended a funeral once of a dear friend and as you can imagine it was a very sad and very emotional event. My ex's expression didn't change it was just like stone. When we were part way through a heart wrenching service I noticed that my ex had water coming out of his eyes, he wasn't crying it was simply like water coming out of the eyes of a statue; it was quite bizarre to watch.

When I was pregnant with our son and I was very happy that I was going to have a new baby I was really excited. I used to go into the baby's room and get out the little baby clothes, I would shout my ex to come and have a minute with me, but he just stood in the door way with an adopted silly grin which made him look retarded. Even when our son was born he didn't change his expression he picked up his new son and he didn't even smile it was just so matter of fact with him, he had a child and that child was like an annoying object to him.

When I tried to talk to my ex about feelings he would adopt a really vacant expression as though he had either shut down from the conversation or he didn't have a clue what I was talking about.

My ex very rarely smiled and when he did smile it would be more of a grimace than a smile he would just put his mouth in a straight line. On all his photos he had the same smile the straight line smile, this smile was on his school photos, on his sister's wedding photos and photos of the pair of us in a shot we had posed for.

My ex had over the years developed fake expressions for certain circumstances. He would when talking to friends or neighbours adopt a silly laugh and he would flap his hands around a bit. When he came home from work his adopted expression would be straight line smile and if I said something jokey he would pull his tongue out a little to acknowledge what I had said, he wouldn't laugh as he didn't think I was funny. If we went out for a meal with friends (of course I had arranged the outing) he would sit with a big fake smile or a straight mouth smile and adopt his silly laugh. He would never initiate conversation with anyone but as my friends and I are loud British northerners his detachment would not really be an issue as we all fought for air space to talk.

1. Does your partner have few facial expressions?

2. Does your partner have a flat effect?

3. Have you noticed your partner has fake expressions for certain circumstances?

4. Does your partner have a vacant expression sometimes?

They have a lot of learned behaviour and coping mechanisms which can hide for a time that they are different.

Learned behaviour

Adults with AS have had to learn certain behaviours to fit in a neuro typical world otherwise they would stand out like a sore thumb and this would leave them open to bullying. They have probably been bullied in the past and realised that they have to behave in way which does not draw attention to them.

People with AS are not stupid they can be very intelligent in a logical way so logic will eventually tell them that the way they are behaving is not accepted. They will look to their peers or television to adopt or learn how to behave in certain circumstances and this in itself can appear odd.

If for instance if someone with AS is with a group of boys and they are all laughing at something but the AS individual does not find it funny he will laugh just so he won't stand out. This is just one example of learned behaviour by studying their peers. One AS man I talked to said he went out with a girl and he noticed that some of the other couples were holding hands, so he held his dates hands, but he didn't let go all night and she became uncomfortable with this and told him so. He said he was confused as he thought that holding your dates hand was what you did, she told him that it was ok to hold her hand but not grasp her all night. On his next date he dropped her hand occasionally and didn't grasp her so hard now he has learned that he can hold his girls hand but not all night and not so hard.

Another lot of learned behaviour is when a AS man (or woman) is dating they will may present themselves as everything you want they may seem sensitive and sweet, kind and loving and they may want to spend as much time with you as possible. You may think you have found the one you want to spend your life with. Then when they have you the sweet sensitive kind man (or woman) will disappear. They have learned or mimicked how they should behave in a courtship but of course this isn't real and the moment they have you they will drop the act as they cannot possibly keep this acting up forever and they become who they really are.

Many NT spouses have said that they didn't know the real personality of their husbands until after the wedding. The wonderful man they thought they had married was gone immediately the AS individual felt it safe to reveal the real them.

My ex had been the most fantastic boyfriend for 10 months of courtship; I adored this gorgeous sweet man of mine. I liked the fact that he was so innocent and a little naïve it appealed to me that he was not a player. What I didn't expect is to have the man who had fallen so madly in love with to simply vanish the day he moved in with me.

My ex used to hold onto my hand when we went out as though he was clinging on for dear life, it wasn't a comfortable hand hold more of a strangle hold on my hand. He used to laugh at things I knew he didn't find funny just to fit in with the crowd we were with, he often said after that it wasn't funny.

My ex used fixed behaviour for most of our life together his behaviour wasn't fluid behaviour like a normal persons would be and which would change depending mood or circumstance. I always knew his behaviour was odd but I couldn't put my finger on what was wrong. I wasn't aware or looking for AS so I didn't put it down to that at the time it was only after the relationship ended and I was so damaged by it that I started to research the hell out of AS and realised that he was a classic case of someone with Asperger's.

My ex had very few friends but he did have one odd friend who shared an interest in the X-box. This friend used to come around to our house every so often and they would play on the X-box until the early hours of the morning. Of course you don't have to have a conversation with your opponent about anything else other than the game you are playing so this was perfect for my ex. In the morning we would sit in our front room and I would usually make them both a bacon sandwich. My ex would sit with me and his friend he would adopt his silly laugh and I would do most of the talking. As soon as his friend had gone the silly laugh and the silly grin would vanish as soon as the front door shut and I would once again be left with a silent housemate.

My ex's behaviour with his son was probably learned from his own father, he was distant and dictatorial with our son just like his own father was with him. I noticed his father was very formal with my ex and my ex was very formal with his own son but then again he was very formal with everyone. The only term of endearment he ever used with our son was buster. He used to say "come on tidy up buster" or "time for bed buster" this way of talking to my son didn't change it was never said with warmth or love it was just something he had learned to say to his son to appear as a normal father. My son now hates the term buster.

Coping mechanisms

People with AS have over the years developed coping mechanisms to cope with certain situations. My ex used to behave in a fixed way in a lot of circumstances he couldn't be fluid like you or me and adapt to different events.

When we visited his parents it was exactly the same format every time. We would drive over to Blackpool where his parents lived and which was approximately 50 miles away in total silence (unless I talked or Adam said something). When we arrived there was the initial fuss over P and Adam from his mum and then there was a cup of tea (very British). After pleasantries we would then have dinner and a desert and then we would sit in the lounge. After sitting in the lounge for a short time P's dad would ask him some computer related question (even though it was me who was the computer expert) and then they would disappear into the spare room for hours talking computers leaving me and Adam with P's mum, leaving me to entertain his mum. Then it was time to go home and we would say goodbye and then drive home in silence. It was always exactly the same the same boring format every time but this was the way he coped with the visit by doing the same thing every time.

P didn't like large social gatherings like special occasion birthday parties or weddings but as I have 30 cousins and there was always some kind of celebration this meant I went alone. If he did come he never lasted the evening he would make some excuse to go home and often I was left alone at parties. I was in a relationship alone, one sided. That was the way he coped with parties, he went home.

P used to use a lot of neutral or ambiguous words when someone tried to talk to him words like "oh yes", "interesting", "go on" he used words that prompted the other person to carry on talking and meaning he didn't actually have to contribute to the conversation. That's how he coped with conversations which were beyond him he laughed a lot and just gave one word answers and when it all became too much for him he left.

One friend of P's emigrated to Canada with his job; after a couple of years he came home to see his friends and family. This friend invited P out to the pub for a drink and P did accept and he did go to the pub but he had one pint and then he came home. I was puzzled when he came home after such a short length of time and asked him how come he was home so soon? He just said I said hello to him had one pint with him and I had had enough so I came home. I couldn't believe that he had not seen his friend for two years and he only spent 15 minutes with him knowing he wouldn't see him again for another few years. His way of coping with a lot of things was to ignore them and disappear.

When P came home from work it was the same every day, he would open the door and I would say hello and I would just get a facial expression from him. Then he would disappear upstairs for approximately one hour which would really get on my nerves as again I was alone with our son. I didn't know he had AS so I didn't know that he was diffusing from the day. P had tried to act normal all day to fit in and he was probably exhausted from doing so and needed this alone time to destress. His way of coping with the day was to disappear and be alone.

Everything seemed scripted with P and it must have been very difficult for him as he just couldn't be himself he had to act his way through life.

P's main coping mechanism was to vanish into his loft room and play on his X-box for hours. He couldn't stand too much noise he couldn't stand company for too long; and if anyone came to visit he would say hello and then he would withdraw into his games room. I was embarrassed when my family visited as he never stayed to talk to them leaving them feeling uncomfortable and unwelcome.

Let me discuss weekends, weekends were like torture for me as P never wanted to go anywhere or do anything he wanted to potter around the house like an old couple. He would concentrate on the house and DIY his way of coping with the weekend and with Adam and me. His way of coping with his little family was ignore us and do work on the house or the garden. The house was perfect the garden was perfect the relationship was lousy.

Another thing I noticed about my ex ASOH was he would constantly run his fingers through his hair when he was in company or when he came home from work. He didn't stim like some aspies do but he did run his fingers through his hair an awful lot.

Some AS individuals turn to alcohol or drugs to cope with the stresses and strains of life. As they suffer so much anxiety alcohol or drugs help in the short term but make things much worse in the long run.

1. Does your partner seem to have a script?

2. Does your partner have special learned coping mechanisms to deal with certain situations?

3. Does your partner struggle in social situations?

4. Does your partner have coping strategies like alone time do they emotionally withdrawal?

5. Does your partner take alcohol or drugs to cope?

No seeking to share enjoyment, interests, or achievements with other people.

My ASOH didn't talk much it was like living with a robot. As a normal person I want to share things with my partner I want to tell them that I have got good feedback at work and I want him to acknowledge that and be proud of me. I want to tell him things I am thinking and feeling and I want him recognise these thoughts and feelings and give me feedback on them.

We are human we need acknowledgment and we need to know that we are cared for and we need reciprocity to live a happy emotional life. One-sided relationships eventually fail as someone leaves because they are tired of being dissatisfied of not being heard of not getting through.

My ex didn't want to spend time with me or his son to be exact he didn't want to spend time with anyone, he much preferred being on his own. He didn't share anything he enjoyed with me and he was not interested in anything I enjoyed in fact he usually dissed anything that I liked.

If we went for a walk which was very rare I would point things out like a baby lamb or comment how beautiful the clouds looked against the sky. In autumn I loved the way the trees changed to so many different colours and I would say how gorgeous the colours looked but my ex was not at all interested the most I would get would be a facial expression or a grunt. My ex would never point out objects of interest he wouldn't comment on something of interest as it wasn't interesting to him.

When we were first together I used to tell him things about my childhood or my wild teens and he would smile but he would never tell me anything about his past. I did think this was odd but I just put it down to him being a little shy, but as time went by I knew that something was very wrong in our relationship but I simply did not know what.

I wanted us to enjoy our son together after all we created him together (with some divine intervention of course). My ex never laughed at our sons antics or praised him for his achievements all the loving came from me. Our child simply received discipline from his father as his belief was that children should be seen and not heard, I did think that in time with my loving influence that he would bend, he did not.

To sum up my ex did not talk about interests or things that had happened in his past or present nor did he share his day with me or his interior life, he did not point out or show any interest in anything apart from his narrow choice of interests. He would spend hours on his X-Box or computer or PSP but when it came to spending time with his family (including his mum and dad) he endured it.

I once was paid for a contract up front and it was quite a large sum of money. I gleefully came home with the cheque and showed it to my ex he took the cheque from me and said "that will pay for us some new wardrobes and windows". That was it he didn't say "well done darling" or "fabulous clever you", I was flattened.

1. Does your partner share any interests with you?

2. Does your partner share there interior life with you?

3. Does your partner point out or talk about objects of interest?

4. Does your partner praise you for any achievements?

Their thinking is rigid they don't have any flexibility they are right and you are wrong.

I love dogs all dogs if they have a sweet disposition (I don't like vicious nasty dogs). If the dog is a Pit Bull a breed which has the reputation of being a very vicious breed but it is sweet natured I would like that dog. My ex hated dogs all dogs he had been brought up to dislike animals, his mother hated animals she thought of them as smelly or annoying creatures at best and she had passed that intense dislike onto her son. My family on the other hand loved dogs we had a dog growing up and she was a big part of our lives.

I wanted a dog really badly so I introduced him to a tiny little Yorkshire Terrier called Pip hoping it would win him over, it didn't . He said that Pip was a smelly horrible thing. Now this little dog wanted him to like it and it went out of his way to make him like it, it followed him everywhere it jumped on his knee it tried to lick him. But he didn't like dogs and he would not change his mind his mind was set in stone and that was that and little Pip had to be returned to my auntie from where he had come.

Rigid thinking is when they have an idea set in stone they will not be swayed or cannot think of the idea in any other way. He didn't like dogs FULL STOP. People with

AS have no mental flexibility or creativity they tend to think of things in one way only. Neuro Typical usually do have creativity and mental flexibility and can look at things with different mental angles.

As for the dog example no dog no matter how sweet or funny or loving would ever change his mind it was made up and he was not going to change it for anything.

P's father was religious he went to church every Sunday without fail, his mother on the other hand was not at all religious she was a complete atheist. My ex had more exposure to his mother when he was growing up; he had a very strained relationship with his father (who I believe had AS too). As my ex was closer to his mother and was not at all close to his father most of his beliefs were passed on to him by his mother and being an atheist was one of them. I on the other hand is not religious but I am spiritual I do believe that there is a power in the universe and I do question why are we here.

On my quest to find answers I have read a gazillion books on spirituality and the afterlife and as normal humans do I tried to discuss it with my ASOH. I don't know why I even tried when would I learn that he had made his mind up and he would never have the flexibility of mind to hear another belief. To him there was no afterlife that was that he had made up his mind I was WRONG.

Another thing which bugged me was my ASOH belief was that the woman cooked even if that woman worked as hard as he did and even if that woman out earned him. I cooked every night and often he would say I don't fancy that I am going to have cornflakes. On the odd night I didn't cook he would ask what was for tea and I would say cornflakes, he was not pleased. When I tried to talk to him about him cooking occasionally he didn't want to know, the woman cooked and that was that.

I was always wrong always always always he was always right I could argue until I was blue in the face he would not budge.

One of our neighbours was out of work after being in the same job for years. When my ASOH asked him why he had packed his job in he said he was being bullied at work. Later that week I was talking to my neighbour's colleague who told me he was in trouble for stealing. As our neighbour worked for the Crown it was a very serious offence and the case was going to go to trial and he was probably going to go to jail. When I got home I told my ASOH this information and he went berserk almost spitting in my face, he said "it's not true who are you going to believe our neighbour or some random man"? I said "it's not some random man I know him and he works with our neighbour and he is very upset about it". He shouted "its bullshit", I didn't bother arguing it was pointless he would not listen. Later that month our neighbour went to prison.

AS sufferers who are argumentative are guilty of not understanding or recognising that their opinions are just that; opinions – and not fact. My ASOH would talk down to me in a tone that implied that he was right all the time and he never questioned that he could be wrong.

When a neurotypical argues with her AS partner the aspie will almost always win the argument or at least have the last word. Because of their nature they will get their own way more often than not. The neurotypical partner will usually down out if sheer frustration and just to keep the peace.

1. Ask your self is your OH always right?

2. Does your OH ever think they could be wrong?

3. Once your partner has made their mind up about something do they ever change their mind?

4. Does your partner ever back down when they think they are right about a subject, even if new evidence is shown to them?

5. Are they always right and you are always wrong?

They constantly misinterpret your feelings.

This particular AS trait drove me insane it used to frustrate the hell out of me. For instance I would be pulling my face as I was thinking about a pile of ironing I needed to do and the conversation would go like this:

P never understood me at all he didn't get me at all even after 13 years together. For instance once I was sat in our front room and I was thinking about a pile of ironing I had to do and I was pulling my face about it. P looked at my face and completely misinterpreted me, you would think that he would know me after the years we had been together and you would think he would know that I am not a miserable or aggressive person. This is how the conversation used to go and it used to drive me mad.

P: What's up with you?"

Me: I am just thinking about a pile of ironing.
P: No you're not you are pissed off with me for going to the races on Sunday.

Me: Am I hell I am not bothered about you going to the races I am thinking about the pile of ironing I have to do and not looking forward to it.

P: No you are not you are pulling your face because you are mad with me.

Me: I am NOT mad with you at all where the hell did you get that from?

P: Why are you raising your voice?

M: I am not raising my voice I am telling you I am not mad with you at all for going out on Sunday, I am thinking about a pile of bloody ironing for god's sake.

P: What are you causing an argument for?

Me: I am not causing an argument (me getting mad as he was telling me how I was feeling and getting it completely wrong)

P: I won't go then I will tell Terry that you don't want me to go.
Me: For fucks sake P I am not mad with you.

P: Yes you are you are shouting at me.

This conversation was a common event he simply could not read my facial expression he used to come up with something completely different to what I was feeling and no matter how hard I tried to tell him he had made up his mind and he would not change it. I drove me crazy.

It didn't matter how much I argued and tried to tell him that I was OK that I wasn't pissed off he would not change his mind. This drove me crazy as it happened often if I wasn't happy and smiley ALL THE TIME then there was something wrong. You imagine trying to keep your face and your behaviour in one mode all the time, imagine how exhausting this would be.

Another example one night I came in from work and I was angry with someone at work as they were being very nasty to me. I walked through the door and put my bags down and said "I have had a shit day".

P : "What's the matter with you?

Me: "A woman at work was being nasty to me and its upset me"

P: "Well don't take it out on me"

Me: "I am not taking it out on you I am just telling you why I am fed up"

P: "Yes you are you are in a horrible mood"

Me: "I am not in a horrible mood I just wanted you to listen while I got it off my chest"

P: "Don't take you bad day out on me I haven't had a good day myself"

I gave up I had learned at this point that he had made his mind up about how I was feeling and he wasn't going to change it. I just went and got my little boy from friends and we played on the PlayStation on Krash team racing while I simmered down and tried not to murder my ASOH.

Another example, P's mum and dad who I got on very well with (well his mum anyway his dad was just another P) were coming to dinner one Sunday. This was unusual, not that they were coming for dinner but that P had arranged it, it was usually me who arranged it with his mum. P told me that they were coming and I said OK that's fine, but my mind was on another subject.

P: "Why do you not want them to come?"

Me: "No it's fine of course they can come"

P: "Well you don't seem very pleased about it"

Me: "It's not that my mind was somewhere else"

P: "If you don't want them to come I will let them know"

Me "Of course they can come; I like your mum and dad why would I not want them to come?"

P: "Because you have a face on" (This is very British for not looking very happy)

Me: "I have told you I am fine I was just thinking about something else"

P: "Well its tough have invited them now"

Argggggggghhhhhhh how annoying do you think this is, it didn't matter how many times I told him I was fine he would not believe me.

These are just three examples of how he constantly misinterpreted me and how he used to tell me how I felt and not listen to how I actually felt, of course he knew better.

1. Does your partner tell you how you are feeling?

2. Does your partner constantly get it wrong about how you are really feeling?

3. Does your partner constantly misinterpret your feelings and they will not change their mind once they made up their minds on how you are feeling? No matter how many times you tell them?

They are Normal

They will make you feel as you are an emotional wreck and they are the normal one.

Oh yes you are weird they are normal it's all your fault as you have feelings. I was constantly reminded that I was up and down and that was not normal, silly me for being human. Trouble is with High Functioning Autism (AS) they appear normal enough for you to have expectations but autistic enough to never meet those expectations.

My ex genuinely believed and still does believe that he is normal and I am crazy, trouble is since he eventually drove me crazy it's reinforced that belief that he is normal and I am the emotional wreck.

When I first got together with my ASOH and I acted like most NT's by showing my feelings but every time I tried to show my feelings or talk about my feelings I was shut out and made to feel I was being unreasonable. For a while I carried on being normal and carried on showing feelings hoping for some kind of reciprocity or acknowledgement, it never happened he made me feel that I was wrong to react or feel like I did. It took a long time of me trying to get some kind of feeling back from my ex but eventually I began to think it was me that was emotionally unstable as he was always on a level therefore it must be me that was not normal.

I started to bottle up my feelings as they were never well received by my ex, trouble is those feelings have to go somewhere and in most cases they turn into resentment and then to depression.

My feelings turned to depression and anxiety and this of course again reinforced to me and to him that it was me who was the unstable one and he was the normal one as he was always on the same level which was either neutral or angry. I was not normal I was crazy, an emotional wreck and totally unstable, I was unreasonable he was normal.

I used to be quite confident in expressing my feelings but as time went by and as my feelings were constantly dismissed as over reacting or being too sensitive or I was being unreasonable, I began to doubt my own feelings. My feelings were never validated ever! I got to a point where I thought I shouldn't be mad with him it's me that has all these unreasonable feelings, I constantly doubted whether I should be upset with him and I thought I must be over reacting and maybe I was being overly sensitive.

I began a very destructive pattern of behaviour; I talked myself out of my own feelings "just let it go Katy"; "don't get mad"; "it's not worth the argument"; "just forget it for the sake of peace"; "don't make it into something big";

you are totally over-reacting again like he has told you a million times".

My feelings whether they were feelings of upset or anger never got quite got quenched or resolved. When I tried to communicate my feelings of upset or anger with my ex-partner he never acknowledged they were justified, he hadn't done anything wrong he was always in the right it was me that was over reacting, how can you carry on like this and stay sane?

As the partnership was so unbalanced and I was quite clearly an emotional nut job I began to feel terrible guilt that I was so mental and he didn't deserve someone who was one tranquilizer away from the looney bin, did he? He was so stable! As a consequence of this I was working overtime trying to fix the relationship, constantly doing things to please him and trying my hardest to make things better trying so hard to make him happier. I felt so guilty and worked so hard to make amends about things that really were not my fault to begin with (only I did not know this at the time).

Over time, you become brainwashed enough to accept that they are the normal one and you are the emotional wreck if you are told something often enough you begin to believe it.

1. Do you feel like you are the crazy one in the relationship?

2. Does your partner point out that's it's you that is unstable?

3. Does your partner seem to be the stable one who is always on a level?

4. Is that level your partner on usually neutral or angry?

5. Do you talk yourself out of feelings?

6. Does your partner acknowledge your feelings?

7. Do you feel like your issues are never resolved?

8. Does your partner point out that he is the normal one?

Exasperating Behaviour.

You will find their behaviour exasperating and even though you will point out why you are exasperated they will never acknowledge that they might be in the wrong.

People with AS can be the most exasperating people to deal with they can very frustrating and will often leave you angry and confused.

After the 'honeymoon' period is over the Asperger's partner will revert to their normal selves as they cannot keep up the acting for too long. And from experience after this act has been dropped depending on where they are on the spectrum it doesn't take long for the relationship to deteriorate. Of course it depends on the NT individual how much they will tolerate and how intolerable the AS partner is before the relationship dies completely.

The person with AS is usually so exasperating , cold and close minded that they will probably bounce from one failed relationship to another , constantly blaming the other person for the failure of the relationship. They simply cannot accept or comprehend that it is their own actions that destroy the relationship they blame the NT spouse for all the problems in the relationship.

One NT Spouse wrote:

I didn't know my ex had Asperger's until he moved in with me and the acting stopped. He was only pretending to be normal behaving so in love with me in the beginning of our relationship and trying so hard not to upset me. Later on he didn't bother faking it anymore and AS reared its ugly head bit by bit, trouble is I wasn't looking for it and wasn't really aware of it at the time. I knew he wasn't wired quite right but I didn't know it was as serious as Asperger's.

My ex was very emotionally retarded and Asperger's really is a severe defect. My ex refused to lock doors even though his house has been robbed. When he is over my house I lock the door and he will unlock the door, when I tell him I want to lock the door in my house he will argue with me. I listen to him telling me in his nerdy voice spouting off crime statistics and how improbable getting the house broken into is. When I tell him just let me lock the fucking door it takes a second he gets a dazed stupid look on his face and looks utterly bewildered and says "why is locking the door so important to you? So I lock the door he unlocks it, I lock the door then he unlocks it.

This is just one of many of the many exasperating behaviours I have to put up with. If I had known he had AS before I dated him I would have run like hell.

Another NT Spouse wrote:

When I told my aspie boyfriend I had strep throat instead of receiving sympathy I got a lecture about the prevalence of it. How annoying do you think this is when you are ill and just want some sympathy and love?

Another NT Spouse wrote:

Everything was my fault I found it so exasperating being blamed for everything, if he smashed a glass it was my fault I had put it into the wrong place. If he drove over the grass getting his car onto the drive it was my fault for parking the car too far over. The blame from an Aspie is unending and completely unfounded everything is my fault, if he dropped a bottle of wine out of the car it was my fault I had not packed it properly.

One thing that used to drive me crazy was when my ex came home from work after hardly greeting me or our son he would disappear upstairs. After a while I would shout to him to ask if he was coming down to sit with me and our son, he would say in a minute. I would sit there getting madder and madder as his indifference to his family and eventually I would shout upstairs "are you coming downstairs to sit with us for bit"? He would eventually come downstairs and sit on the other sofa away from me and our son. I used to say to him come and sit with me and Adam (our son) and he used to say you look really comfy, I gave up asking in the end.

I remember asking my ex to teach our son to ride a bike, I asked him and asked him and still he didn't take any notice. I would have taught Adam to ride his bike but I wanted him to spend quality fun time with his dad as my ex didn't do anything with Adam. I was trying to encourage a better relationship between them and to create some nice father son memories for Adam. Then one day I was really getting annoyed with him with this bike issue and I said to my ex "for god sake will you teach Adam to ride his bike before he gets too big for it, all his friends can ride a bike and Adam is being left out". My ex reluctantly took Adams bike out of the garage and he took the pedals off it so Adam could get used to the bike as a balance bike (the best way to teach kids to ride a bike). As he was teaching Adam how to ride his bike he started to clean his car at the same time while keeping a scant eye on Adam. Adam was shouting "daddy am I doing good"? He was so excited but P (my ex) was too interested in getting his car cleaned and hardly noticed Adam. I was furious with P but I had learned at that point that it was totally pointless telling him that Adam wanted his attention and his approval as he simply didn't understand this. As far as he was concerned as he was teaching Adam how to ride his bike wasn't he and that was what I wanted wasn't it? My poor child he never received what he need in terms of love, warmth, affection and approval from his father.

One incident stands out in my mind when Adam was about 8 years old he said to me "mummy do you know me and you have a laugh and I really love you" I said "I love you too my darling" he said "it's not like that with my daddy he is a bit like (he screwed his little face up trying to find the right words) a stranger to me, can we sit down and talk about it" I was flabbergasted that a child of 8 could be so perceptive.

I have always said to Adam that if anything was bothering him ever that we would always sit down and talk about it and sort it out and this was his way of trying to "sort it out" with his dad. I dug a little deeper and asked him what he meant, he said he doesn't want to play with me mummy he just wants to play with his friends on the x-box and he just wants to get me in bed so he can play with his friends. I was heartbroken that my child felt this way. When P came home I said your son has something to say to you. We sat down and Adam said to his dad what he said to me (while partially hiding behind me) and P just said well I will have to try harder, and that was that. As a normal loving parent I would have been devastated with this statement off my child but not P he simply said I will have to try harder.

1. Do you often find yourself frustrated and exasperated by your partner's behaviour?

2. If you point out your partner's behaviour do they accept that they could be wrong?

3. Do you often find yourself confused and bewildered by your partner's behaviour?

They may not like kissing or hugging. They may "act" affectionately in the beginning, but they will not be able sustain it.

When I first met P he was very affectionate always hugging and kissing me, he used to reach out and touch my hair all the time saying it was soft and silky. After the honeymoon period was over and his "normal" façade dropped he hardly hugged me and he never kissed me unless it was a peck on the lips.

P never gave me spontaneous cuddles or kisses they always came from me and when I did cuddle him he used to put his whole body weight on me like me hugging someone who suddenly dies in your arms and becomes a dead weight. This bugged the hell out of me and I stopped hugging him as I had told him countless times that he was too heavy to put all his body weight on me and besides I didn't find it nice cuddling a dead body.

When I had spoken to P about how unhappy I was as he didn't show me love and affection he would try for a while but even when he was trying it was so forced, he used to order me to kiss him as I passed him. He would point at his lips and make a sound like mmm mem and I would dutifully go and give him a peck on the lips, but even this he didn't keep up he would revert straight back to no kisses or cuddles.

When we went to bed and I tried to cuddle up to him he would move to the other side of the bed facing away from me as he didn't like me breathing in his face and he said he got too warm. After a while of being rejected every time I tried to cuddle him I gave up trying. As other things in the relationship deteriorated bit by bit, criticism after criticism one stupid misunderstanding after another and a boat load of negativity to go with it eventually there was nothing left between us but a gaping gap, I gave up totally and left.

Some people with AS don't like unexpected cuddles or touching if they know about it beforehand they are prepared for it and will accept another's touch. Some do not like light touching they only like a firmer touch.

1. Does your partner not like being touched?

2. Does your partner not like kissing?

Sexually Robotic

They are often lacking passion and are very rigid, repetitive, and robotic or technically perfect in bed with no passion or emotional connection.

Sex was pretty good when I first met my ASOH but after a while when he felt he didn't need to impress me anymore it became routine and robotic. What my ex didn't understand was he had to be nice to me before I would have sex with him, he couldn't be horrible all day and then expect me to fall willingly into his bed and perform. As sex was just an act to him just to satisfy him he didn't have a problem having sex even when things were shit between us, but I did.

Even when things were going OK between us the sex was very robotic and there was no kissing or intimacy between us it was simply an act. P was only interested in satisfying his own needs he really didn't care about mine so I was always left unsatisfied.

I knew when P wanted sex as he would come behind me and twiddle my nipples, I don't know where he had learned that from or why he thought it was foreplay and when he did it I wanted to turn round and punch him as it really irritated me. He sometimes used to come and put him head on my shoulder from the back and push his privates into me and make silly grunting noises like he was thrusting, I found it revolting and a massive turnoff. I asked him once would he like it if I came behind him and stuck my hands down his pants and started to rub his penis and he looked at me disgusted and as though I was crazy.

I am by nature a bubbly loving, tactile and sociable creature and I like sex, not with anyone of course I tie it closely with love. P didn't understand that he had to be nice to me to get a session, he would be his usual flat boring criticising self all day and then come behind me and twiddle my nipples and then when we did go to bed he would be stuck to my like leech with one hand on my boob I sometimes ignored him or sometimes to get him off my case I would have sex with him. He hadn't been nice to me all day but I couldn't explain this to him as he would just go off on one and say I was never happy, it wasn't worth the anxiety it would add to my life.

We did have lots of spontaneous sex when we first met until he moved in with me and then it stopped and like everything else just became a routine. He wasn't bad in bed but he wasn't interested in my needs just his own. Sex was a boring frigid routine where he would do the exactly the same thing at the same time and when he had climaxed (usually far too soon) that was it finished done all over leaving me aggravated at his premature ejaculation.

I stopped trying with our sex life as he was embarrassed when I tried to be sexy making me feel not at all sexy just stupid. A man once said to me does your husband tell you that you are beautiful every day? I said my husband would not notice if I pranced around in front of him naked with tassels on my nipples he would probably say get dressed you look stupid.

My mum and dad lived in Spain but came home every so often as they still had a house about 4 miles from me. When my dad went out it was easier for him to stay at my house, so I would often find him asleep in my spare room some Saturday mornings hung over and fully clothed! It didn't bother me at all my dad staying but P said your dad can't stay again I don't like it. It took me months to get out of him why? He said you won't have sex with me when your dad is in the next room (no shit Sherlock) so he can't stay. What he couldn't understand is it was him that had created this routine of Saturday morning sex as he had rejected me every single time I tried to be spontaneous with sex that I had totally given up and by that time I really had become to detest P. He had put sex on the Saturday morning routine rota and it couldn't change from this as it didn't "fit in" with his routine at any other time, it didn't matter whether I felt like it or not this was "his" routine and he did not want my dad to spoil it.

P was not asexual as some aspies are he did want sex sometimes, he didn't want spontaneous sex it had to be at certain times. P was technically good in bed but there was simply no connection at all between us he could have been having sex with a large side of beef

1. Is sex robotic?

2. Do you feel any emotional connection during sex?

3. Do you have spontaneous sex or does it have to be planned?

4. Does your partner find your touch irritating?

5. Is your partner asexual?

My ASOH had very narrow food choices when he was growing up he would only take chocolate spread on white bread sandwiches for school every day for all of his infant school days. At home he would only eat chips or cornflakes and of course chocolate spread sandwiches. I asked his mother once did she not try him with different foods she said it wasn't worth the battle it would cause.

When P was in his early twenties his sister got married and had a big white wedding. P would not eat anything off the buffet or at the meal so his mum went to the reception of the hotel where the wedding was and ordered some chips for P.

When I got together with P he would eat other things apart from chips and cornflakes but his food choices were still narrow. P would not eat fish and he hated the smell of it, if I cooked salmon he would heave as though he was going to be sick, so I stopped eating salmon. I often cooked a roast dinner and my choice of meat would vary, some weeks I would cook chicken some weeks I would cook lamb or beef. I had to stop cooking lamb as he said it tasted too strong.

I didn't know at the time that P had AS so I just put it down to him being a fussy eater but later on I learned that aspies have sensory issues like smells, tastes and touch and their senses can get overwhelmed by any of these, so it made sense that P didn't like strong tasting or smelling foods.

Research also tells us that many individuals with AS tend to have strong preferences for carbohydrates and processed foods, while rejecting fruits and vegetables. This is probably as they have an aversion to strong tastes and textures.

P did get better with time he would try new foods and sometimes he would like them and sometimes he would throw it away and get some cornflakes. My diet did get less varied as he was such a picky eater and it was too much trouble to make two different meals at tea time I tended to just cook what he liked.

1. Is your partner a picky eater?

2. Does your partner prefer carbohydrates and processed food?

3. Does your partner not like strong smelling or tasting food?

4. Are your partner's food choices very narrow?

Soft Clothing

They often don't like inflexible clothing or the feel of labels on their skin.

Sensory Processing Disorder is something that most AS (high functioning autistics – aka – Asperger's) suffer from or SPD for short. Some suffer more than others for instance they are hyper sensitive to all the senses some are only hyper sensitive to some of the senses.

My ASOH was over sensitive to touch and texture he couldn't stand wearing jewellery (he thought it looked gay too) he said it scratched his skin. He used to say certain clothes irritated him, he used to sleep in the nude as the riding up and twisting and bunching of his pyjamas drove him mad. He didn't like clothes that didn't move with him like stiff shirts or jackets; he hated wearing a suit and a tie he said he felt like he was trussed up like a turkey.

I remember him always wanting me to cut the labels out of clothes as he said they scratched him. I have a vision of him in my head standing there while I cut the labels out of his tops while he was wearing them.

P hated shaving with a passion he said it made his face sore but he had to shave as he couldn't grow a beard as it grew with bald patches, but he would have done if he could. He had very dark hair so his stubble would show through very quickly so he had to shave every day. At weekend he would often go without showering and shaving and I would go mad at him saying he looked like a tramp, he would say I am giving my face a break. I didn't like it as he looked nice every day for work and at weekend when we were supposed to spend time together he looked unkempt and scruffy.

When I look back I now see that most of P's clothes were soft fabrics like soft t-shirts and soft hoodies or smooth knit jumpers under which he would put a vest as he said the jumper rubbed his nipples. When he came home from work he would disappear upstairs for ages (that's another topic) and when he came down he had often changed into some lounge wear which consisted of soft trousers and a soft top somewhere in-between pyjamas and a tracksuit.

At the beginning of our relationship I would buy P presents for birthdays and Christmas sometimes it would be clothing like a smart shirt and some smart trousers and he would take them back every single time so I swapped to buying him aftershave or trying to get out of him in a subtle way what he wanted and it was often a game for the Xbox or surround sound for the Xbox or a gaming chair for the Xbox, I gave up in the end as if he wanted these items he was selfish enough to buy them anyway.

P was sensitive to certain textures too; I bought a soft throw for the bed and he couldn't stand touching it, he said it went through him (made him cringe for you folks outside the UK) and he got rid of it. He hated fur (I only bought faux fur) and if I tried to cuddle him with one of my fur trimmed jackets he pushed me away as he couldn't stand the feel of the fur.

1. Is your partner sensitive to certain textures?

2. Do you or your partner cut the labels out of your partners clothing?

3. Does your partner prefer soft clothing?

4. Does your partner complain about certain clothing being irritating?

They can be hurtfully honest and very critical.

Brutal honesty

There is honesty and there is brutal honesty, Aspies usually possesses the latter. Aspies are brutally honest trouble is sometimes honesty and the truth can be very hurtful or simply piss someone off. Aspies seem incapable of telling a white lie to protect someone's feelings.

Aspies are so compelled to tell the truth and they simply do not have the capacity to foresee how that truth might upset the person's feelings, you will be upset sometimes by their seeming insensitivity.

If you ever want to know if your backside looks to big in an outfit, just ask your AS partner!

As a neurotypical we know sometimes we have to tell white lies to protect other people's feelings if we were brutally honest at all times we would just be labelled as rude. Aspies don't have this filter and will often come across as rude and insensitive.

P was very charming and sweet in the beginning of our relationship and said all the right things so imagine my surprise when he moved in with me and things changed literally overnight. I was left with this blunt, negative and critical man who became a stranger to me.

I would get ready for a night out and come down stairs to show him how nice I looked and he would say I don't like that top it's too glittery or I don't like that fur on that jacket it's over the top. I would go from being quite happy with the way I looked to feeling self-conscious with my appearance.

I remember coming home from the hairdressers having had my hair cut into a new style and feeling really pleased with the result. I walked into the house and found him (on his Xbox) and showcased my new style, asking him at the same time did he like my new hairdo? No it was better before was his reply, I was utterly deflated.

It was my job to make tea every night which I did sometimes begrudgingly, I often tried new things which I had seen on TV. P's response was not always kind he would say "yes that's ok you can make that again" or "I can't eat this crap".

P eventually wouldn't pass an opinion on anything I would ask him if he liked my new hair colour and he would say I am not saying anything as I can't have an

118

opinion it's always wrong so I am not saying anything. All these "little" things contribute to the failure of an AS/NT relationship, it's not so much anything really big which is the downfall of the relationship its lots and lots of little things which chip away at something which seemed so solid to begin with. Imagine not being able to discuss anything with your other half as he won't say anything for fear of being wrong.

Constant criticism

I struggled every day with my ASOH arrogance and my powerlessness to convey my feelings about his constant criticism I eventually became silent and considered leaving him (for years). I couldn't get through to him so I shut up as I didn't have any other option either shut up and put up or leave. No other option seems available to me.

When I tried to tackle him about him criticizing every little thing I did and every little thing about me he just thought I was being unreasonable and deliberately causing an argument. It drove me crazy I simply could not communicate to him how he hurt me with his nit picking.

I couldn't ever do anything right for him, the way I parked my car to the music I listened to (it was shit apparently). I didn't put the dishes in the dishwasher correctly, I had drove over the corner of the grass with my car, I hadn't put the cutlery in the draw properly, and I had put the bin out for the binmen and I had not put it far enough down the path. I bought Adam a helmet for his bike and it was crap and he looked a bugger in it, so he went out and bought another. This constant negativity and constant criticism took its toll on me eventually and I became less and less confident and I constantly doubted myself and my opinions, I lost who I was.

Constant criticism and constant nit-picking he couldn't ever say anything nice to me, he couldn't compliment on anything, he never said I anything nice to me. He treated me like I was stupid even though I had a very good job as an IT instructor and out earned him.

As Adam got older and he needed me less highlighted the gaping holes in mine and P's relationship, I dreaded being with him as it was bloody hard work like walking on egg shells, I had to constantly be aware what I said and to think about what I said before I said it as it could possibly cause an argument as he took it the wrong way, keeping the peace was so hard. I began to avoid him wherever possible and the sex virtually stopped as he thought he could be horrible to me all day and then want to have sex with me at night, he didn't understand that to have a good sex life you have to actually like your partner and I began not to like him at all so why would I want sex with him?

He didn't like the way I dressed, I am a fancy pants and I love diamonds and frills and fur and anything glittery, he like plain. I got ready to go out one night and I had a black frill trim dress on it was beautiful and I said do you like my dress? He said it would be nice without that stupid frill?   I said it's a fucking frill trim dress, god how I hated him. Do you like my new coat? I don't like that fur collar he said, it's a fur collared coat and without the fur it was nothing. I have got a new top do I look nice in it? It's a bit glittery isn't it? It's a glitter trim top, well I don't like the glitter. Do you like my hair I have put it up? No I don't like trussed up hairdos.

I said to P once do you actually like me at all as I feel like I am just an irritant to you? Of course I do stop being paranoid he replied in an annoyed tone. And that is exactly how I felt Adam and I were to him just an irritant, it beats me why he stayed when he obviously did not like me at all towards the end. But still I tried as I kept thinking I might eventually make him like me again if I was thinner, prettier more interesting earned more money etc.

1. Does your partner constantly criticize you?

2. Do you feel like you cannot do anything right for them?

3. Does your partner nit-pick at everything you do as though they do it much better?

P was cold and distant and very insensitive to my needs and our son's needs, his needs came first every time. I truly believe he did not act this way out of selfishness I now know he simply could not fathom the needs of a normal wife and a normal child.

When I lost my dad suddenly I was devastated and I looked to my ASOH for comfort but he didn't comfort me he withdrew from me. Looking back he withdrew from me as he didn't know how to deal with that level of emotion, he was OK with me when I was happy but he couldn't understand me when I cried or when I was excited about something. P didn't feel these levels of emotion or if he did he did a very good job of behaving like Dr Spock.

I remember crying once as I felt so overwhelmed by everything, working being a mum looking after the house, trying to keep fit and attractive (I thought he would love me more if I was slim and attractive) and having very little time to myself. I just felt very emotional and I cried which in itself is very unusual as I do not cry easily, instead of putting his arms around me to comfort me he just looked at me as though I was mental. I so very much wanted him to hug me and tell me everything was going to be alright and that he was there for me, but he didn't he just looked at me crying.

When Adam was a toddler about 2 and half years old he had a bad cough and he couldn't stop coughing, his little body was wracked with coughing and his chest rattled. A little girl who lived near us was in hospital with meningitis and she had nearly died, luckily enough because of the actions of an experienced paramedic who gave her massive doses of the right drugs she lived and was absolutely fine. As a consequence of this I was paranoid about Adam getting meningitis and I watched him like a hawk especially as he did play with this little girl just before she became ill. I said to my ASOH "can you sleep in Adams bed and let him sleep with me I am so worried about him"? P knew all about the little girl nearly dying but he simply did not understand my angst and he replied "I'm not sleeping in a single bed and he will be alright he just has a cough". I was so worried about Adam I squashed at the side of him in the single bed and cuddled him all night waking every so often to check he was still breathing. I know I probably overreacted but I was petrified that something would happen to my darling little boy, but P let me and Adam sleep in a single bed together with my little boy ill and P slept in the double bed on his own.

P did not ever meet any of my emotional needs I was starved of love and affection he was completely mind blind to mine or Adams needs. Adam is now 14 and he is angry towards his father and he remembers quite clearly being emotionally rejected by his dad and the sad thing is he is still being emotionally rejected by him. P has no idea how to meet the emotional needs of anyone including his normal teenage son.

P was totally insensitive to his mother too but she had been married to P's AS father for years so she was probably used to the indifference. His mother would call every week and P would say a few words to her and then pass her over to me, I used to tell him that it was her son she wanted to speak to but he would still pass her over to me every time she rang.

My ex father in law who I believe has AS has a fascination with America, he would not holiday anywhere else. My ex mother in law has a bad heart and it cost them a fortune to insure her for holidays and the travel to America is too much for her. In fact one of the times they were on holiday in America she had a heart attack and was hospitalised for most of the two week break. But my ex F in Law still insists on dragging her on a 20 hour journey to America even though he knows it could kill her and despite asking him countless times to holiday in Spain where the travel would be a couple of hours he simply will not holiday anywhere else.

This used to baffle the hell out of me why can he not see she cannot handle the travel, why can he not see how she feels why is he so god damn selfish? Why is he so insensitive to her needs, can he not see her discomfort.

I was talking to my ex mother in law once about holidays and she said it was her dream to go to the Italian lakes for a holiday. I asked her why she didn't go and she said that my ex F in law didn't want to waste money on a holiday he wouldn't like and that he would only spend money on going to America as he enjoyed that.

P would never show any sensitivity to anyone or anything I told him that next doors cat had died and he just shrugged. This little cat was adorable and he used to sit on either mine or P's car every day and purr until we stroked him. The cat was called Eric and we had seen him every day of the 10 years we had lived in the house and I had grown quite fond of him so I was upset when he died but P didn't give a damn.

1. Does your partner show any sensitivity to your feelings?

2. Does your partner seem like Dr Spock when it comes to dealing with sad occurrences?

Seek out time alone when overloaded by people.

P needed a lot of time out but as I didn't know he had Asperger's at the time I thought he was just being ignorant. When P had been at work all day he would come home and I would greet him with a cheerfulness I didn't feel but if I didn't greet him like this he would withdraw even further into himself.

When P came home from work and after the initial play act of being pleased to see him and after asking if he would like a brew (part of the act) and he usually said no, he would disappear upstairs and would be playing around with either a PSP/Computer/Xbox for what seemed an age. Adam and I would be sat on the sofa watching some rubbish Adam liked, I would be getting angrier and angrier the longer P was upstairs I kept my anger to myself as I didn't want to start a row in front of Adam and I didn't want to go through another row and then a period of us dancing round each other awkwardly until I apologised as he never apologised as he couldn't see what he had done wrong he said it was my fault I was being unreasonable. Eventually I would get that aggravated I would go to the foot of the stairs and say nicely what are you doing love? What I wanted to say was "why don't you get your fucking ignorant arse down here and interact with your family you inconsiderate wanker" I never did say that (but boy it was on the tip of my tongue many a time) I was always polite to keep the peace.

When P eventually came down, still in his work stuff he would sit awkwardly on the other sofa as though he was a visitor, and I would say come and sit here with me and Adam, he would say you look comfy I will stay here, if he did sit with us it was stiff and uncomfortable and he didn't stay long, it was anxious time for me as it felt like I was sat with a dead body.

I only realise looking back that this time upstairs was time out for P as he had spent all day trying to fit and act his way through the day in a neuro typical world. It's a shame that I didn't know this as I could have at least tried to understand his needs and realise he needed this time to diffuse from the day.

Time out didn't just happen when P came home from work it happened at lot and it always happened when he had been in the outside world for instance at a party (which he hated attending). If we did attend a party or a function he would make his excuses and go home and when I eventually returned home he would be sat in his man cave (the loft room) on his X-box.

If we had visitors which was another contention in our house as I had a big extended family which would drop in

129

unannounced, this was something that all the family had done all my life and we were always welcome. P's family would meet by arrangement only, you simply did not turn up at his mum and dads house and if you did you would be told it was inconvenient at that time (it wasn't on his AS fathers schedule). P found this difficult to accept and was often rude when my family came and he would disappear upstairs and leave my family to me. When I confronted him about it he thought it was rude to just call off at our house without an invite. I told him that this was my house too and that I wanted my family in my life and that they were always welcome. My family were not so inconsiderate that they called off at ridiculous hours and they did not overstay their welcome it was usually a cup of tea and a chat and then they were on their way.

In the end we compromised as I said to him that I was never rude to his mum and dad and I always made a big effort with them and all I asked was that he greet my family and stay just for a little while and then he could go and have his alone time.

If P went out with his friends which he rarely did as he could not sustain long lasting friendships unless the other person made the effort, he would be back within a couple of hours and then he would go up to his loft room and play on the X-box for the rest of the night, often until the early hours of the morning.

P needed a hell of a lot of time out and alone time and I now know he desperately needed this time just to diffuse and to be himself.

1. Does your man often spend hours alone?

2. Does your man need time out after work?

3. Does your man need time out after parties or functions?

Often they do not seek or need comfort from other people.

P never came to me to talk about anything that was bothering him so I never knew what he was thinking or if he was in emotional pain. If seemed to be annoyed about something (which was often) I would ask him what was the matter, he never ever told me what he was feeling and badgering him to get to the bottom of his mood was a waste of time he would simply withdraw further.

After the initial courtship and after he had moved in with me I was puzzled by his day to day behaviour as he didn't share his day with me or talk to me about what was going on with his life outside the home. As I was completely unaware P had AS and as a NT person would, I tried to initiate conversation with him but was met with one word answers which was very frustrating.

I couldn't fathom why he didn't talk to me and didn't share his feelings with me, why he didn't need any love or affection from me. This left me feeling very unwanted and unloved and I would ask him if he did love me and he would answer in a very annoyed tone as though I was just being a pain "of course I do I have told you before haven't I?". This response did nothing to alleviate how I felt as it was delivered in such a way that made me feel pathetic and needy.

Every normal person has ups and downs in life and most people turn to friends or family for comfort. I was feeling upset about a woman at work who was bullying me and as any normal person would do I went to the person who was supposed to be the closest to me, P. P was not at all interested and he didn't give me any feedback on the situation he just looked at me with a vacant look on his face. The bullying from the woman at work carried on and it began to really upset me and it got as I didn't want to go in work as the atmosphere was awful, again I spoke to P to see if he could give me any comfort. P just said go to Human Resources and report her, which I was going to do anyway but in the meantime I wanted some words of comfort from him, but there were none.

P NEVER turned to me for comfort for anything I knew nothing of his interior life, I only knew the shell, the outer man, the inner man was never shown to me. I know that P didn't talk to friends about any feelings as he didn't have many friends and the ones he did have he rarely saw.

1. Does your partner ever seek comfort from you or anyone else?

2. Do you not know the interior life of your partner?

They cannot read facial expression or body language and will often interpret you wrongly.

It is widely known that people with Asperger's and autism have trouble reading other people's facial expressions. They will be able to read basic emotions like happy and sad, especially if they are exaggerated.

I have read a study which states that as much as 80% of communication between humans is nonverbal. This means facial expressions and body language between humans is way the majority of communication is carried out. Imagine how hard communication would be if you couldn't read facial expressions and body language and you were totally unaware of it? It would almost be impossible wouldn't it?

Many people with AS are not aware of their own facial expression and usually they look angry or upset. One of the most common comments people with AS get every day are "Are you angry with me?" or "What's wrong?" and "Cheer up!" because many people with AS have a consistently neutral facial expression. This can make people feel very uncomfortable because they cannot read what the other person is thinking. It can also make the person with AS seem quite unapproachable, even if they really like the other person and really would like to talk to them.

P struggled enormously with facial expressions he couldn't read me at all he constantly read me wrong. I Would be perfectly happy but not have a smile on face and he would insist that I was unhappy about something, and no matter how many times I told him I was OK he would not believe me. This drove me crazy as he would tell me how I was feeling and I would tell him how I was actually feeling and he would not believe me he KNEW how I was feeling better than me!

Communication with P was near to impossible as he would not divert from his perceived impression of events and I could have told him until I was blue in the face and he would not change his mind.

I lost my dad suddenly and very unexpectedly and it knocked me sideways, I was devastated. One of my aunties had suffered with anxiety and mental ill health and she gave me some tablets to numb the way I was feeling. I knew I was stupid taking the tablets but how they made me feel (numb) was better than the overwhelming grief and anxiety I was feeling. I took the tablets on an empty stomach as I was not eating at the time, and later on I had a glass of red wine. Two sips of the red wine and I collapsed and P had to drag me unconscious to bed, I don't remember a thing. P called the ambulance which took ages to come and by the time they had arrived I had come to a little. The paramedics wanted to take me into hospital but I would not go, I stayed in bed most of the following day.

After this event P ignored me for days and when I asked him why he was ignoring me he said that I had taken the tablets and collapsed "for attention". I tried to explain how bad I felt about losing my dad (6 weeks prior) and I took the tablets to numb the pain and that I didn't bank on collapsing. P said no you didn't, you took them for attention. I tried and tried to tell him but he would not listen he said I could not have been that upset as I had been fine all day!

My relationship with P was difficult he would ask me if I was angry or upset and I would say no I am not angry or upset. He would be so far away from the truth of the situation but insist he was right and then he would get annoyed with me when I would deny that I was feeling the way he thought I was feeling! He would say that I was being untruthful and he could not understand why I was not telling the truth arrghhhhhhh.

P would be horrible with me all day and when we went to bed I would lie with my back to him as far away as possible. If P wanted sex he would try to cuddle up to me and place his hand on my breast, I would take his hand off my breast and move further away. Any normal person would read this body language and know that I was upset with them and either ask why or turn away and go to sleep. P didn't get it and he would keep cuddling me until I either gave in and had sex to keep the peace or I would go and sleep in the spare bedroom citing a headache.

P simply could not read situations, facial expressions mu body language or anyone else's or that matter and it made my life very difficult and I bet it made his life difficult too.

1. Does your partner often read your facial expression and get it completely wrong?

2. Is your partner unable to read body language?

3. Does your partner make up their mind about a situation and get it completely wrong but insist they are right?

They might have very formal manners.

I used to think that P was just a quiet old fashioned gentle man who had been taught to behave correctly at all times. If we went out to dinner he would hold himself rigidly and speak very formally, he would not be relaxed and use humour with me or the waiting staff.

If we went to a BBQ at a friend's (which was not often) he would stand stiffly with a beer in his hand and adopt a goofy laugh, not once in all the time I knew P did he crack a joke or use any kind of humour or sarcasm. P was polite to the point of complete stiffness at all times.

P held himself stiffly, spoke with very formally he used to greet all his friends and his male relatives with a stiff handshake and he always without fail greeted them with "hello sir" it didn't matter who they were it was always "hello sir" it could be his dad, his brother in law my uncles the greeting did not change. When he greets females he just said alright? I didn't think about it at first I just thought he was an old fashioned gentleman. But now looking back on it and with the certain knowledge that P has AS this strange stiff greeting was something he had learned and he never strayed from it as his greetings cannot be made with warmth and or change to fit the relationship with the recipient.

Even at home when we sat together as a family he would hold himself stiffly and be polite and correct at all times, I can only liken it to living with an android that has been hard wired to be polite, formal, correct and stiff at all times.

Even when we had sex it was a very formal event with no passion or emotional connection, he was very good technique wise but it always left me feeling like he could be having sex with a side of beef and not the women he was supposed to love.

1. Has your partner got very formal manners?

2. Is your partner very rigid and stiff in many different circumstances?

3. Do you feel like you are living with a shell of a person?

4. Do you feel like one day you might break through the wall and get to the person underneath?

Emotional Invalidation

If you try and tell them about a problem they will not be supportive or reply with a statement that invalidates your feelings.

Emotional invalidation is when someone's feelings are rejected or ignored, it is very hurtful to be emotionally rejected and it's particularly hurtful for someone who is emotionally sensitive. Being constantly emotionally neglected in a relationship creates a distance between you which if not addressed will never be closed.

P was constantly rejecting me emotionally and it made me feel worthless.   Like any normal person I am up and down, life is like that no one goes around being fantastically happy all the time, shit happens. P used to tell me that I was not normal and that it was not normal to be up and down and why could I not be like him and be on a level.

P most of the time had neutral face and sometimes I would tell him something that you would think would evoke an emotional response and I used to get was a vacant expression. Sometimes I would get a short comment or sometimes I would get no comment, it made me feel confused and invalidated.

I would wrap my arms around him and tell him I loved him and he would give an embarrassed laugh and walk away, this rejection really hurt me.

I had an argument with a kitchen fitter who had fitted our new kitchen for us and he had made a mess of the work. I was very upset when I came home from work as the kitchen was a complete botch job and we had paid a lot of money for it. My mum and my mother in law were in the kitchen when I got home and they both looked at the kitchen with a horrified expression and looked at me for my reaction, I cried.

I was so upset I rang the kitchen fitter straight away to tell him I was not happy and he was sacked, P was in the back ground going mad as he thought the kitchen was OK. I couldn't believe he would think that the mess which was the kitchen was OK and we could live with it. I was not going to pay £20,000 for my dream kitchen just to "live with it". He was not happy that I had sacked the kitchen fitter and he went mad at me and told me to sort it out as I was overreacting. The following day I rang another company and they came and took the whole kitchen out and refitted it to perfection. P never ever backed me in anything he contradicted everything I said and everything I believed.

I worked for myself as a freelance IT instructor and even though I enjoyed my job it was very exhausting. I used to tell P how exhausting the job was being on your feet all day, keeping the delegates entertained and interested as well as delivering some complex subjects. He used to say it's not anymore exhausting then any job; my job is just as exhausting as yours. One of my friends who had worked in training told P that she found the job very hard work much harder than a desk job. P would not listen he rejected my feelings and ignored my emotions as far as he was concerned I was talking rubbish.

P ridiculed a lot of my beliefs he ridiculed my spiritual beliefs to a point where I didn't even mention them anymore. The silly thing is with my beliefs that they are just that my beliefs I didn't ridicule him not believing in anything spiritual I just thought he was entitled to his opinion.

P blamed me for everything he blamed me if he smashed a glass it was my fault as I had put it in the wrong place. If there was a mark on the paintwork in the house it was my fault, he even said that he thought I marked the wall just to piss him off!

P even used to invalidate me with body language like rolling his eyes or just by completely ignoring me. I was crying one day as I felt overwhelmed by everything (I was probably hormonal) but he said "what are you crying for?" when I told him he rolled his eyes and walked away.

1. Does your partner blame you for everything?

2. Does your partner invalidate your feelings with body language?

3. Does your partner tell you that you are over reacting when you know you are not?

4. Does your partner dismiss your beliefs?

5. Does your partner dismiss your feelings?

If you end the relationship some many forget about you immediately and even replace you with someone else right away like changing a car. Some may continue to pursue you for a long time.

Walking away without a backward glance

At the end of the relationship with someone with AS they will either move on without a backward glance or they will hang on and pursue you for a long time.

At the end of the relationship with P I had totally had enough I was exhausted with trying to keep him happy and keep the peace. I had to end the relationship for my sanity and for the mental health of our child. I was done trying to make him happy, I used to think I wasn't thin enough, pretty enough, interesting enough, I just thought I wasn't enough. The sad thing is that I now know that no matter what I did he was NEVER going to be happy he had Asperger's.

The day before we split up we had been to a funeral of a friend and had a big argument at the funeral and he was not speaking to me AGAIN.

The following morning we sat in silence in bed and then he said "we are going to my mums tomorrow to see the kite festival". I groaned and said "I really could do without it I am really busy" (the truth was I didn't want to spend the day acting as though everything was OK and playing happy families). He got up out of bed and said "well we have to make an effort with my parents you know". He stormed off into the shower and then went downstairs.

I showered at a leisurely pace not in the least perturbed by his outburst as I really had had enough of him at this point; I got dressed and then went downstairs to do some work on my online shop. I was sat at my laptop working and P stormed past me and said something, I said "sorry I didn't catch that", he went to go out of the front door and he popped his angry head back and said "I have told my mum you are too busy tomorrow so there that's your get out clause you don't have to go". I said "well actually I was going to go but it doesn't matter now does it" (secretly relieved). He then went off to get his hair cut and I stayed at the computer mulling over the day before and then this morning.

P arrived back home and he bristled past me obviously fuming with me. I completely ignored him I didn't care anymore I just carried on working. P went into our sunroom to watch something on the television and I was thinking about my life or lack of life with him and something in me snapped.

I got up from the computer and went into the sun room and said to him:

Me: I'm done

P: what with work?

Me: No with you I don't love you I can't remember the last time I loved you, I don't even fucking like you, that's it over finished we go our separate ways.

P: You are not getting this fucking house.

Me: I don't want this fucking house and that says it all doesn't it, that your first words are not I love you and Adam so much please don't leave, no your first reaction is you are not getting this fucking house.

I ignored him for the rest of the day I felt very calm almost serene I had done it I had finally gone and done it, all those years I had thought about it and planned the day I would leave and now I had actually done it.

I moved into the spare room that night, and the following day P asked Adam was he coming with him to the kite festival and our Adam said "no I am staying with my mummy", so off P went to his parents to watch the kite festival with them. I slept in the spare room for a week and he slept in our room and when we were not working and were in the house together he was in the loft room while I was downstairs.

I think he thought I was just having a tantrum and that I would come around, but my mind was made up this was it I had finally had enough of him I hated him despised him I wanted to punch him every time he opened his stupid mouth. How the hell had it come to this?

After a week he realised that I wasn't coming around I wasn't having a tantrum and I wasn't going to apologise. I said I wanted him to leave and he said he wanted to stay and sort out our problems but at this point it had gone too far I had put up with him for far too long and I just wanted out. He went a week to the day after I told him it was over and all I felt was relief. I thought I might be upset or think what the hell have I done have I made a mistake but all I felt was lighter and free.

At first he was very angry and he wouldn't speak to me he moved all his clothes and possessions out of the house I asked him could we at least be friends but he shouted that he would be civil with me and that's all. Not once did he say he loved me and not once did he hold me in his arms and display any kind of heartbreak. I rang him once in tears and said I really didn't want it to be this way and he said well it's the way it is and it was your choice again NOTHING back from him. He just could not see that it was his behaviour which had drove me to this, he thought he had done everything right and I was ungrateful and unappreciative of all his efforts ha ha bloody ha.

After a couple of months P started to text me asking if he could do anything to fix it. I kept replying no you cannot fix it don't you see I can never do anything right whatever

I do is wrong, you criticise my every move, so no you can't fix it. One day when we were still on speaking terms he rang me and he was crying, I was still not aware he had AS at this point so I thought my god he does love me he is crying. I told him to come over after work and we would talk. I genuinely thought he had learned a lesson and things could be different now.

He came to our house and he sobbed in my arms and tried to kiss me, I let him kiss me and after he said to me "that kiss still meant something didn't it" if I am honest it didn't mean anything to me but I am so soft and I didn't want to kick a man while he was down so I said "yes it did". Even then my heart was full of dread as I didn't want to go back to how it was but as I was still unaware of P having AS and indeed AS in general and their complete inability to change. I thought he may of learned a lesson, I really thought it might be better this time, we had a house a child and a history together so it might be better this time, my god how stupid of me and how wrong I was.

We started to date again and it was OK not great but OK at least he was being nice to me, I knew he would never be the life and soul of the party or a chatter box I knew he would always be quiet but at least he was being nice to me and that after years of emotional neglect and abuse felt good. Eventually I told him that we were never going to know if it was going to work out between us again if he lived 50 miles away so would he like to move back. His answer knocked me for six, he said "not this week I am too busy with work" WHAT THE HELL too busy with work are you kidding me you were crying two week ago begging me to come back. I couldn't believe my reaction either I should have just told him to go to hell but I heard myself saying "when do you want to come back then"? He said "next Friday".

What had just happened there I thought one minute he was sobbing in my arms and begging me to come back saying he couldn't live without Adam and me and then he was telling me that he was too busy to move back, yes I was confused once again.

P moved back into the family home and he first night he moved back he came in through the door and he didn't look happy to be back I kissed his cheek and said welcome home he just smiled a gimpy smile. The first morning after he move back we were sat in bed drinking a cup of tea and I said to him I better clear out your wardrobe to which he replied in a annoyed tone "I thought you would have done that already" I just looked at him and thought what the hell have I done.

What struck me after he moved back that there was no sex he didn't try to have sex with me he didn't try to spend any time with my or Adam he spent most of his time working in the office which was in the loft. P was worse than ever more horrible to me more ignorant than ever I was really puzzled to why he would beg and sob to come back and then be horrible to me when he did come back?

I went out with my friends on a champagne lunch and imbibed too much champagne I came home a bit pissed but I am not a nasty drunk so I wasn't being horrible when I got home. Adam and P were sat in the front room and I just said drunkenly "I think I had better go to bed" his face was like thunder and I wondered what the hell I had done now but I was drunk so I went to bed. When we woke up in the morning you could have cut the atmosphere with a butter knife and I felt the old anxiety rising in my stomach he wouldn't look at me he wouldn't talk to me he just withdrew into his angry passive aggressive shell. I thought WTF is going on here again I was bewildered.

A couple of days later after barely seeing him as he was working from 8 in a morning until 9 at night and then going to bed I was sat downstairs on my own yet again. I started to sing the song all by myself at the top of my voice; I only did it to make him laugh, would I ever learn he thought I was stupid he didn't think I was funny. I went upstairs and said "did you hear me singing to you"? He turned around and he was fuming really angry and he shouted "yes I did and I am sick of you taking the piss" I was shocked at the anger in which he spat these words at me, I said "OMG I was only joking P, I was just trying to make you laugh". He said "no you were not you were taking the piss" I tried to talk to him to make him see that I was only joking to lighten the atmosphere but he was having none of it he maintained that I had done it to piss him off.

The following day I was back to where I was before confused, upset, anxious and totally perplexed at what had happed since he came back. I said to P "well we are back here again aren't we" he screamed at me "it's your fault I want someone who doesn't come in drunk and who doesn't take the piss out of me" he screamed "I want someone **normal**" I said normal you want someone normal it's you that's not fucking normal and what you really want is someone who doesn't have a personality or a sense of humour and who doesn't have a damn thing about them at all and that's not me so piss off back to your fucking parents' house" . He deliberately caused this massive argument so he could leave and once again I was bewildered what the hell had gone on here what the hell had I done or not done AGAIN I seemed to spend my life feeling like this.

P went back to his parent house unbeknown to me he had met a 28 year Polish girl in-between begging and sobbing to come back to me and moving back. P went straight into a relationship with her he had deliberately been horrible to me and caused a huge row over nothing so he had a reason to leave and so he could go straight to her. He wasn't in love with me he wasn't ever in love with me I was just a caretaker to his needs he only wanted to come back as we had a nice house and we were both relatively well paid. He kept this secret from me as he wanted the money out of the house and he knew if I found out I would hit the roof.

When the house was sold he called off at my friends who he had not contacted since we split just to tell her that he had a girlfriend and she was 28 and he had been with her for 6 months and that he was really happy. This visit to tell my friend was of course was just so it would get back to me. When it did get back to me I was devastated not that I wanted him back I didn't but that he could move on without any feelings or backward glance, it cut me to the bone. I had tried and tried and put so much effort into the relationship for years and I was now so scarred from that relationship that it will probably affect any future relationships and he could just move on completely unaffected completely unscarred that's what hurt so much that I meant so little to him.

I can only liken living with P to living with a robot which has been programmed to have a neutral to negative outlook on life and programmed to get up in a morning go to work, work come home, moan, criticise constantly play on the X-box, clean and tidy up and have sex occasionally. He was also programmed to ring his mum and dad once a week and say virtually nothing on the phone which left his poor mum to think of something to say to him to which she received one word answers.

It's no wonder I ended up so utterly unhappy, anyone who is normal would be unhappy living with an android device. My son said "he is an android mum and not a good one like a phone which you can at least interact and play with" I thought this was funny and perceptive and that came from my 12 year old son unprovoked.

I only began to realise that P had Asperger's after my sister gave me an article out of the Daily Mail about living with a partner with AS talk about ringing bells. When I read the article my sister and I looked at each other and she said "that's P isn't it"? I said yes. I have researched this for 3 years and there is no doubt in my mind that P has AS.

P moved on without a backward glance and that hurts really bad as I now know I should have trusted my gut instinct years ago when I used to think he doesn't love me he just puts up with me as he likes his lifestyle.

Hanging on for dear life

Lorraine who was married to a partner with Asperger's for 7 years ended the relationship with her husband but he would not accept it.

Lorraine moved into the spare room and made moves to divorce her partner. He made threats to kill himself and he started to act very bizarre. He started to stalk Lorraine; she would turn around and see him hiding behind a bush pretending he wasn't there. She would be shopping in the local shopping mall and she would see him darting behind posts and into shops when she turned around. When Lorraine confronted her ex ASOH he denied that he had even been to the mall.

Lorraine said it was a long and drawn out process to get rid of her ex-husband, Lorraine she said she felt cruel and heartless and then she remembered the years of emotional neglect and the lack of participation in her or her children's life and her resolve to end the relationship strengthened.

Lorraine said that she came home from work two years after her divorce to find her ex-husband in her living room. Lorraine was shocked and then she noticed that her computer was on and that he had been looking through her emails and social media pages. The AS partner's explanation was simple and honest "I want to know what you are saying about me to other people."

Lorraine said that he still referred to her as his wife 10 years later.

1. Has your partner moved on without a backward glance?

2. Has your partner left you heartbroken and doesn't seem to care at all?

   Or

3. If you have ended the relationship is your ex having great difficulty letting go?

Email me with any errors you find in this book and if you want to send me your story. Let's get it out there about these types of relationships and lets help the poor NT spouse, there is enough help for people with AS and Autism lets help Neuro Typicals.

mailto:katyadamford2002@gmail.com?subject=My Story or Error in the book

Printed in Great Britain
by Amazon

84742862R00092